I0037866

CREATIVEKEYNOTE

7 Keys to Public Speaking Artistry
for Creative Professionals

HEDLEY DERENZIE

Creative Keynote: 7 Keys to Public Speaking Artistry for Creative Professionals

A Pinecone Book

First published in Australia in 2016

By Pinecone Publishing

Copyright © Hedley Derenzie 2016

All rights reserved. No part of this publication may be reproduced, stored in a retrieval system, transmitted in any form or by any means electronic, mechanical, photocopying, recording or otherwise, without the prior written permission of the publisher.

Derenzie, Hedley, 1978 –

Creative Keynote: 7 Keys to Public Speaking Artistry for Creative Professionals

A Catalogue-in -Publication is available from the National Library of Australia

ISBN: 978-0-9875508-3-5

Pinecone Publishing

A division of The Galt Group Trust

Sydney, Australia

CONTENTS

INTRODUCTION   7

Key 1: Purpose – What's yours?   17
A Useful Definition   21
Different types of public speaking   24
Public speaking is an act of service   26
Claiming the role of public speaker   29
The Big Question   33
What's your 'why'?   36
Purpose is cornerstone of power   38
Remember, people buy why   41
Crafting your Purpose Statement   42
So let's get real   46

Key 2: Prepare to Be Yourself   49
We are born original   53
Original gifts   56
'Be yourself, everyone else is taken'   59
There is no comparison   61
Your relationship with fear   63
When fear isn't really fear   66
Shame   68
Acknowledging the one in 'fear'   70
Just Be (with) Yourself   73
Loving the skin you're in   74
Your body is your instrument   77
Cultivating a healthy mind   78
Engaging presence   82
The source of power   83
Practising presence (not perfection)   85
Practising conscious breathing   88

Key 3: Plan Your Content   91
Seek first to understand   95
Freedom through structure   96

The Keynote Map   98
The Introduction – The Gift Wrapping   100
The Creative Grab   102
Your personal story   104
Setting the Scene   105
The Middle – Three is Key   108
Conclusions – Tying the Bow   110
A quick summary   112
An invitation to act   112
An emotional anchor   113
Questions and answer time   113
Managing your time   114

Key 4: Personalise Your Points   **117**
The purpose of storytelling   121
Becoming a storyteller   127
The willingness to be vulnerable   129
Accepting the risks   132
Sharing our personal stories   135
Personal versus Private   136
Engaging visual aids   137
The dark sides of slides   139
Changing the way we use slides   140
Be Creative   143
Your greatest visual aid   144

Key 5: Practise Your Delivery   **147**
Be the audience member you want as a speaker   149
Practising presence not perfection   152
Ditch the script   156
Preparing our instrument   159
Vocal projection   162
Maintaining your energy   166

Key 6: Present Your Keynote   **169**
Personal preparation   173
Keynote preparation   176
Environmental preparation   177

Working with technology   178
Listen to your audience   180
Listen with your senses   182
Let go of outcomes   185
Coping with Criticism   187

Key 7: Prosper Through Speaking   **191**
Become a professional speaker   194
Seek out opportunities   195
Build your speaking portfolio   197
Create a Speak Sheet   198
Promote yourself   199
Finding an agent   201
Getting paid   202

CELEBRATE   **207**

Resources   210
Next Steps   211
Acknowledgements   212
About the author   213

INTRODUCTION

Poised and ready with the microphone in my hand, I flicked my hair behind my shoulders as I waited as patiently as I could for Joe to manoeuvre his commercial-sized television camera into position. This was going to be a blast. After all, I was born to be a television presenter. Well, that's what I was thinking when I agreed to the gig. I've always loved talking to people, asking them questions and finding out what makes them tick. Surely doing it in front of a camera while holding a microphone would be much the same? This could open doors to a whole new world of opportunities. Yes, this was going to be a walk in the park; my ticket to the big time. If only we could just get moving. What on earth was taking him so long?

Joe looked up from behind the camera, signalling he was ready to go.I straightened up, took a deep breath, and brought the microphone up to rest just under my chin. The moment had arrived. Finally I got to hear that long awaited word:

'ACTION!'

The red light flashed on and…

It was 1999. I'd been living in Los Angeles for almost twelve months, having arrived with nothing but a backpack and a sense of freedom unlike anything I had ever experienced before. I could do anything. At least, that's how it felt. For the first time in my life, a world of infinite and exciting possibilities was opening up to me. Opportunities presented themselves in ways that appeared effortless and miraculous. If I thought, *Hey I'd like to give that a go*, whatever 'that' was would somehow show up in my life. It was a magical time.

I had always wanted to try my hand at writing. One of my friends who worked as a Fashion Director for a Californian fashion magazine put in a good word for me with the editor. Next thing I knew I was venturing off to Hollywood parties and fashion shows and writing about them for the paper. Television presenting had always looked like something fun to try. Sure enough, while sipping on a margarita at a party and watching the sun slip behind the Malibu mountains, I struck up a conversation with an attractive blonde woman who turned out to be a producer for a local television cable station.

'I'm always looking for new on-air talent,' she said. 'How about coming by the station next week and we can see how you go?'

By the time I walked through the glass doors of CitiCABLE 22's studios the following week, I had my entire future mapped out. This was going to be my big break, my ticket to fame and fortune (not to mention a US Green Card). No matter that I had no previous experience, relevant training or qualifications. I just figured my natural and outgoing personality would suffice.

'CUT!' yelled Joe, the sound of his voice jolting me out of my trance.

I looked around at my surroundings, confused and wondering, *What just happened?*

Whatever did just happen certainly wasn't what was supposed to happen. Never mind. Just a minor mishap. I shook my head and steadied the microphone. Beginner's nerves, I told myself. Nothing to worry about. Joe repositioned himself behind the camera as I stared into the large black hole of the camera lens. Joe signalled to go.

'ACTION!'

Once again, the red light flashed on and once again my life flashed before my eyes. My heart thumped hard against my chest, my throat contracted and my mouth went dry. I tried to speak but no sound came out. By now my mind had gone blank. Completely blank.

'CUT!' yelled Joe, this time with a tone of slight annoyance.

'I'm really sorry,' I told Joe. 'I don't know what's wrong. I guess I just freaked out.'

Joe nodded and I could have sworn I saw him roll his eyes as he let out a long sigh and began resetting the camera. I took another long, deep breath. *C'mon Hedley. There's nothing to worry about*, I thought to myself. *Just relax. It can't be that hard. It's just a camera.*

Joe signalled for me to go again and again, as the red light flashed on, my body betrayed me; my mind went blank.

'CUT!' he yelled, this time offering some half-hearted encouragement. 'Try not to think about the camera. Pretend as if you're talking to a friend.' I nodded while staring back into the dark and cold lens that looked anything but friendly. 'And don't forget to smile.'

Of course! How could I forget to smile despite being completely and irrationally terrified? I plastered a wide grin on my face and told myself that this time I was going to get it right. Unfortunately the positivity didn't last long.

It took Joe twenty-one takes to get a decent one. Not a great one. Not even a good one. Just a decent one. I was thankful when the day was over. As we began packing up, I felt discouraged and disappointed. My high hopes at becoming a wonderfully well paid, not to mention legally working, television presenter had been well and truly dashed. I had thought I would be a natural in front of the camera. I thought this was going to be my ticket to the big time. How could I have been so wrong?

It's been almost two decades since that moment I crumbled in front of Joe's camera in Los Angeles, and a lot has happened in that time. Upon arriving back in Sydney, one of the first things I did was enrol in a public speaking course. As terrified of speaking in front of others as I clearly was, my fear didn't make sense to me. Nor was it acceptable to me to remain in this state of fear for the rest of my life, because speaking in public was something that I was going to have to do at some point. Little did I know at the time that my desire to overcome my fear would lead me into a career of helping others to do the same.

Over the years I have done almost every course on public speaking there is to do. I've also facilitated many such courses as a contract trainer for various companies. Every course, whether I was the participant or the facilitator, brought me one step closer to becoming more in control of myself when in front of an audience. Yet there was always something missing in these courses. After over a decade of running other people's programs and talking about other people's philosophy, I wanted to take my public speaking, and the speaking of those I was coaching and training, to a deeper level.

I travelled to Santa Fe where I participated in an intimate public speaking program that really helped me to define and connect to my own personal philosophy about what it really means to be a public speaker. And what I discovered was significantly different to all the courses I had run in the past and all the books I had read on the topic. I started putting my ideas down on paper and this eventually turned into my first book on the craft of public speaking, *Real Raw & Original: An Authentic Approach to Public Speaking*. Having always been a passionate writer, publishing a book was a lifelong dream and it was a wonderful to bring my two passions – writing and speaking – together in this way. Yet something odd happened after I published the book – people expected me to be this perfect and polished public speaker even though this was exactly the expectation I was attempting to change and redefine.

I found it difficult to shake this expectation. The thing is, I've never been naturally comfortable or confident in the spotlight and I'm anything but perfect and polished when it comes to speaking in public. Yet nor am I trying to be perfect. After many years of studying the craft and developing my own philosophy, principles and methodology, I have come to understand why public speaking is important and it's got nothing to do with perfection and looking good in front of others. Instead, I believe that the opportunity to speak in public is about having a defined purpose and hopefully making some kind of difference. Ultimately, that is what this book is about.

The truth is I still get nervous before speaking and I even had this experience recently at a friend's engagement party. When it was time for the speeches, my friend nodded to me across the table, inviting me to stand up and say a few words. Even with a few wines under my belt, I froze except for my head, which was vigorously shaking from side to side, my non-verbal response that said, 'Oh, please no. I love you and I wish you both much joy and happiness in the years to come but for God's sake please don't make me stand up and say that in front of everyone.'

The girl seated next to me knew I had written book on public speaking and elbowed me in the ribs.

'C'mon, you're the expert public speaker,' she whispered, or at least thought she had whispered but may as well have stood on her chair with a megaphone, since everyone at the table looked over at me with intimidating expressions that I read as, 'So you're an expert public speaker, huh? Well let's see about this!'

I quickly discovered there's a difference between writing a book on public speaking and doing the public speaking. I'm far more comfortable writing than I am speaking, but it's this fear of public speaking that has enabled me to come to such a deep understanding of what it means to speak in public. By claiming my role as a public speaker, through both writing about it and doing it, I now understand that public speaking is an act of service where I have a far greater capacity to help others and to make a difference in my own unique way. My goal is to help others come to this same understanding and thereby transform their approach to and experience of speaking in public.

Much has happened since publishing my first book and I'm more passionate than ever to change the way we approach the craft of public speaking. As uncomfortable as I used to be (and sometimes still am) on stage under the glare of the spotlight and hundreds of pairs of staring eyes, I know I'm there to serve a higher purpose than my own perceived need for validation and approval. As long as I maintain my attention on that purpose, I'm less likely to be stymied by the fear of what others may or may not think of me.

These days, whenever I speak in public, I'm speaking from a place of greater awareness and acceptance of the person I am in that moment, which inevitably is a greater version of myself than I was yesterday. I bring that expression with me to every situation I engage in, whether it's writing a book, speaking in public or simply hanging out with family or friends. I'm no longer trying to be perfect: instead my intention is to bring more of who I know myself to be to the present moment.

I've by no means cured my fear. It still exists within me. However, it no longer overwhelms me or prevents me from speaking. Eventually I did stand up and say a few words at my friend's engagement and as always, once I got over those initial seconds of inner torture, I felt fine simply because I maintained my focus on the reason I was speaking in that moment, which in this case was to celebrate and honour my friend's happiness.

Public speaking is about being of service rather than being perfect. There's no such thing as a perfect public speaker anyway. This book is not about being or teaching people how to be a perfect and polished public speaker. It's about unravelling everything that stands in the way of being yourself in front of an audience and seeing the act of public speaking as a platform to express ourselves in ways that can uplift, inspire, enlighten and empower. Speaking in public is a fantastically powerful vehicle for inspiring others and for changing people's lives, including our own.

Key 1
Purpose – What's yours?

I come as one but I stand as 10,000.

DR MAYA ANGELOU

My public speaking journey began in Assisi, a small town in Italy set amongst the rolling green hills of Umbria. Not that I knew I was embarking on any such journey at the time. I was eight years old and my only concern at that point was which flavour of gelato I was going to choose for my afternoon treat. My family and I were in the middle of a three-month holiday around Europe, mainly encompassing Italy and Greece. One place my parents particularly wanted to visit was the Basilica of San Francesco d'Assisi, otherwise known as the Church of Saint Francis, located in the small Italian town of Assisi.

Naturally I wasn't that interested in visiting churches. Not only did they look exactly the same after a while, I had already established that religion wasn't for me. Even though I was raised Church of England, attended a religious school and partook in Sunday school and other religious occasions, I felt uncomfortable in these environments. Religion, including the teachings and the incessant rituals, simply didn't make sense, nor feel right in my body. While adults still had the power to tell me what to do, no one had the power to tell me what to think. That was my private domain. Of course, none of this made any difference to my parents and my protestations for having to visit yet another church fell on deaf ears.

Upon entering the Basilica of San Francesco d'Assisi, my sulking and whining stopped. Beneath the magnificent golden archways, a deep sense of peace came over me. Immediately I became enamoured with this man called Saint Francis and I found myself wanting to know everything about him. *Who was he? What did he do? Where did he live? When was he born? When did he die? Why are there so many people here paying their respects to him?* It was as if I could feel the presence of this man within me, as if he somehow knew me. Standing amidst the glorious interiors of this sacred place, I could feel Saint Francis's love surrounding and embracing me. I felt warm and safe in the presence of this energy. It was as real as the centuries-old mosaic floor on which I stood.

Upon returning to school, the principal asked if I would be willing to share some details of my trip during morning assembly. Excited, I immediately agreed, wanting everyone to know about Saint Francis and to experience the gifts that I had experienced since becoming aware of this beautiful, kind-hearted saint. I thought the perfect way to do this would be to read the Prayer of Saint Francis, one of the many treasures I had acquired during my magical visit to the Basilica, as they were words which had resonated more deeply with me than any prayer I had recited in the past.

There was no sense of fear as I walked to the centre of the stage in front of five hundred plus children and teachers, including my Year Three peers. Silence encased the large school hall as I placed the piece of paper with the prayer on it on the podium and took a moment to adjust the microphone. After briefly introducing myself and explaining what I was going to share, I looked up at my audience and began.

> *Lord, make me an instrument of Your peace.*
> *Where there is hatred, let me sow love;*
> *Where there is injury, pardon;*
> *Where there is doubt, faith;*
> *Where there is despair, hope;*
> *Where there is darkness, light;*
> *Where there is sadness, joy.*
> *O Divine Master, grant that I may not so much*
> *Seek to be consoled as to console;*
> *To be understood as to understand;*
> *To be loved as to love;*
> *For it is in giving that we receive;*
> *It is in pardoning that we are pardoned;*
> *And it is in dying that we are born to eternal life.*

As I finished reading, I turned and raced off the stage, my face flushed and my body wracked with shame. During the reading of the prayer, from somewhere at the back of the hall, I heard the faint sound of giggling. As I continued reading, the giggling became louder while catching on with more and more kids like an infectious disease. As the laughing gained momentum, so did the waves of humiliation that crashed down around me as I stood at the podium. By the time I had finished the prayer, many of the kids were struggling to contain their laughter while the teachers struggled to regain order. Backstage, I was left to deal with the shock of having the gift I had so enthusiastically wanted to share with others – one that was so deeply personal – thrown back in my face.

Although I didn't know it at the time, my fear of public speaking was born.

A Useful Definition

I like using the term 'presenting' when I'm talking about public speaking because it's a reminder of what it is I'm really there to do – to give to the audience.

The term 'presenter' originates from the Latin word *praesentare*, which means 'to place before'. When we present something to someone, we place it before them. Put more simply, when we present we are there to give – not just information and knowledge, but ourselves as well. Presenting is an act of service through the opportunity to offer something of value.

Medieval legend says that when someone presented a gift to a person of a higher standing they would bend down on one knee, and with a bowed head raise the gift up above their heads, in honour of the person they were kneeling before. Whether or not this is true, it's a wonderful image that I like to hold in my mind when thinking about speaking to an audience. Even though I might be standing up on stage, my intention is to create the experience for the audience that I'm offering my gift in honour of them. My presentation then becomes more like an offering than just another scripted speech.

When we approach the act of public speaking from this perspective, we start to forget about all the tricks and tips for getting what we want from our audience. Presenting is not about convincing, manipulating or forcing something down people's throats. Nor is it about whacking up hundreds of slides and rattling off some boring facts in the hope that we can get our presentation over and done with as quickly as possible.

Our purpose as presenters and public speakers is to use this opportunity to make an offering of value to our audience, presenting our offering in a way that invites our audience to engage with us by listening to our message and exploring the value it might create in their lives if they were to accept it. In the same way we share our art with others, we are sharing our message and ourselves.

No, this doesn't mean we literally have to position ourselves on bended knee with our heads bowed and hands lifted over our heads. We are simply shifting our view off worrying about what we can get from our audience, to focusing on what we are there to give. When I shifted to this new, more generous perspective of public speaking, I quickly discovered my whole experience of public speaking transformed. When we are in a state of giving, something wonderful happens: we forget ourselves. When speaking in public, this can really come in handy.

By taking our attention off ourselves and placing it onto what we can do for our audience, we take our attention away from whatever fear and anxiety we might be feeling. Instead of worrying about what we look like, the judgments our audience may or may not be making, how to sound impressive, trying to remember everything we have to say, not making any mistakes and a whole host of other concerns, our attention is simply focused on the act of giving and anxiety turns to healthy excitement.

Giving feels great. When we are in a state of giving, we are more closely aligned to our most authentic version of ourselves. With our attention focused on what we can do to make some-one else's day better or easier or more enjoyable, we seemingly forget our own doubts and fears and limitations. It matters not if we are standing in front of two people, a hundred people, a thousand people or a television camera – every time we stand before an audience, we always have a choice: we can speak from a place of selfishness (what can I get?) or selflessness (what can I give?).

Fear becomes simply an indication that we are focused on ourselves and meeting our own needs rather than focusing on others and making an offering. When we choose to use pub-lic speaking as an opportunity to be of service, we make the choice to no longer be victim to our fear. There is a way to do it differently. I know this because I have made this choice and I continue to make this choice every time I speak in public. It's a conscious choice that has freed me from my own fear. As a result, a miracle happened: I actually started to enjoy speaking in public.

Different types of public speaking

*Nothing liberates our greatness like the
desire to help, the desire to serve.*

\- Marianne Williamson

Before I began studying the craft of public speaking, the image that my mind conjured up about this act always involved a large room, a large crowd and a lonely speaker standing on a stage behind a podium with the spotlight beaming on them while they looked completely terrified. Essentially, this one and very limited definition was supposed to encapsulate this notion of speaking in public. Needless to say, it wasn't a very enticing definition and it's no wonder I spent so many years avoiding having to do it.

After gaining a more in-depth understanding of public speaking, I came to realise that public speaking is far broader than I realised. In fact, public speaking is a very broad term used to describe the many different ways a person can deliver a message to an audience. Understanding the different styles and methods of public speaking available to us can help reduce the anxiety we might be feeling, while also relieving the pressure we may have on ourselves as the kind of public speaker we believe we have to be.

A presentation can be a casual affair involving someone standing or even sitting at the front of the room having a conversation with a group of people, or a more formal speech involving more of the scenario I painted in the previous character. Yet public speaking can also include facilitating a workshop or training program, delivering a sales pitch to a potential customer, promoting a new book to a small group in a library, pitching a script to a movie studio, asking a question following some-one else's presentation, giving an educational talk to a group of school kids or even just presenting an idea to a small group. Put even more simply, public speaking is a vehicle for delivering a message to a group of two or more people.

A 'keynote' presentation is generally considered a more formal style of public speaking, involving a speaker standing up on stage delivering a well-prepared speech to a willing audience. While there is great value in being able to deliver this kind of presentation, this book is about expanding our definition of public speaking beyond the formal approach to one of authenticity, connectedness and individuality. A 'creative keynote' presentation is one that still maintains the basic premise of a speaker and an audience but which incorporates the unique and creative expression of the speaker.

If public speaking is something that you are afraid of or resistant to, then my suggestion is to examine your definition of public speaking. Is it limiting you and your experience of public speaking? What do you believe about public speaking and are these beliefs supporting and encouraging you to engage more in the act? If the answer is 'no', I recommend you start challenging your own beliefs and definition and start to create new ones.

Public speaking is an act of service

Over the years, as my understanding and experience of public speaking has matured, I have come to believe that public speaking, or presenting, *is an act of service.* This belief alone has changed my entire experience of public speaking to be a more positive and enjoyable one and any time I find myself speaking in front of a group of two or more people I engage with this idea.

When I took my first presentation skills workshop all those years ago, I had no idea of the journey I was embarking on. I thought I was collecting a few tips on how to be a more confident speaker so I could stand up in front of a group of people without falling over. What I discovered, however, was far beyond anything I could have ever have imagined.

After a couple of years spent participating in presentation skills workshops, an interesting, if not surprising opportunity presented itself. A friend of mine who worked for a corporate training company had a presentation skills course coming up with no one to run it. Knowing that I had become slightly obsessive about doing public speaking courses in an attempt to stamp out my ongoing fear, he asked if I would be willing to step in as a facilitator.

Me? Teach people about presentation skills? You've got to be kidding!

The request didn't entirely come from out of left field. At the time I was working for a modelling agency and I had recognised that the models and actors I was representing could use a little help in the confidence department. I designed a three-hour workshop which I then facilitated, giving them all the knowledge and confidence needed to make it in a highly competitive and cut-throat industry. The workshops were a hit and I discovered that facilitating workshops (as opposed to keynote speaking), was something I was quite good at. Plus, I really enjoyed it. I told my friend I would be happy to facilitate the presentation skills workshops for him.

On the morning of my first workshop, I arrived absurdly early in order to set up the training room and prepare for the participants who would soon be arriving. Only three people had registered for the course, which I was actually happy about. The small number slightly took the pressure off my nerves. C'mon, I was petrified. Although I had gained enough understanding and skills by then to not allow fear to sabotage me in the same way it had in Los Angeles. At least, that's what I hoped.

With only a few minutes left before nine o'clock I paced the empty room, wondering when someone was going to arrive. The longer I waited, the more nervous I became. I was anxious to get started, as I knew once through those first few minutes, I would be fine. Breathing deeply, I continued to pace, up and down, up and down. Fifteen minutes later, the room was still empty. By the time nine-thirty came around, it was clear that no one was coming. My very first presentation skills workshop and not one person showed up. I couldn't have been more relieved. In fact, I was elated. Especially since I was still getting paid.

Of course the day came when someone did show up for their workshop and I was called to get on with what I was there to do – help people become more confident public speakers. The nerves continued rattling away inside me, but once I got going I quickly discovered that I was happy people were showing up and that what I was doing was much more important than simply getting paid. I was helping to change people's lives for the better.

One of the biggest surprises I received during those early days of my career was that there were people in the world who were more afraid of public speaking than I was. In fact, there were lots of people who, like me, wanted to face their fears and overcome them, knowing that to do so would liberate them both personally and professionally.

The people who attended my workshops desperately wanted to be better presenters. They were overcome by fear in the same way I had been in Los Angeles and that simply wasn't good enough. They wanted to understand themselves, to better themselves because on some level they knew that this goal was attainable. They knew, perhaps not consciously at that point, that they did possess the ability to be inspiring, engaging and memorable public speakers, even though they had no evidence of this just yet. It was the courage of the people attending my workshops that inspired me to continue doing this work.

As I began helping others, I realised something strange was happening. I felt my own confidence developing. The more I helped others, the more confident I became. I'm certainly not suggesting that my fear vanished and I no longer felt nervous when I spoke in front of a group of people, but I could see there was a purpose for public speaking greater than my own need for validation and approval. I was doing something that was adding value to people's lives.

This realisation was so immensely gratifying that my purpose started to become more powerful than any fear. My passion for giving people the tools and confidence to overcome their fears dissolved much of my own. I started to go beyond my own issues and see public speaking for what it actually is – an opportunity to make a difference. And as a result I started to see my role as a presenter as more than just a job for which I got paid, whether or not people showed up.

As we've already discussed, the role of the presenter simply means 'to place before'. When we present we are 'placing before' both ourselves and the message we are there to share. While how others respond to our message is outside of our control, our intention to make a difference is not. And when we present, we are there to make a difference. We are there to offer something we believe is of value. This is our purpose and when we connect to our purpose, we go beyond any fear we might be experiencing.

Claiming the role of public speaker

One of the first questions I ask my clients when they contact me is, 'So are you a public speaker now?'

They will usually offer a response along the lines of, 'No way! I'm definitely not a public speaker. That's why I'm contacting you. I want to learn how to be.'

I will then rephrase the question. 'Have you ever spoken in public before?'

'Of course,' they will say. 'I give presentations at work all the time, I spoke at my sister's wedding. I've spoken in public many times.'

'So you're a public speaker then?'

'No, no. I'm definitely not a public speaker.'

I remind them that I didn't ask them how good they are. I'm simply asking if they are a public speaker. Okay so it's a trick question, but the reason I ask this question is to highlight one of the biggest mistakes people make when it comes to public speaking: they don't see themselves as a public speaker; they haven't claimed the role of a public speaker. And if you don't see yourself as a public speaker, it's very difficult to improve as one.

Imagine you're a parent but you go around telling everyone you're not a parent based on the fact that you're not as good as you think you should be. It simply doesn't make sense and it just wouldn't happen. If you have a child, then you are a parent. Of course the kind of parent you are is entirely up to you.

It's the same with public speaking. If you want to improve as a public speaker you first have to be a public speaker. To be a public speaker, you simply have to claim it. So how do you claim something? This is perhaps the easiest thing you could ever do. You claim the role of a public speaker simply by stating: 'I am a public speaker.'

This statement alone will change your experience of public speaking for the rest of your life. It is perhaps the most important step toward becoming a public speaker and it's also the easiest. If you have ever stood up in front of a group of more than two people to speak, no matter what the topic is or how long you spoke on it, then you are a public speaker. Plain and simple.

This is a huge shift in perception for a lot of people. With almost everyone I have ever worked, hardly any saw themselves as a public speaker. Not initially, at least. Having them claim this role, based on the fact that at some point in their life they had stood up in front of a group of people to speak, immediately shifted their energy around public speaking. Take a moment to see if that's the case for you. Close your eyes and say to yourself a few times: 'I am a public speaker'. How do you feel when you say that? What is happening inside your body as you repeat those words? Are you in agreement with this statement or do you feel the resistance? Remember this is not about what kind of public speaker you think you are. You're either a public speaker or you're not. And in my experience, everyone is a public speaker.

The good news about claiming the role of public speaker is that it's not based on opinion. It's a fact. It's just another one of the many roles you play in life. And as you start to get comfortable with this new fact, you can start to explore yourself in the role of public speaker as you move about your day.

In the same way an actor explores a role in preparation to playing it in a movie, you can start to get to know what it's like to play the role of the public speaker. How does a public speaker walk down the street? How do they get dress in the morning? How do they eat breakfast, mix with their colleagues, enjoy a home cooked meal for dinner? By simply asking the question,

'How might a public speaker do this or that?' the answer will reveal itself through you.

You might even notice a shift in your behaviour. You might find yourself adjusting your posture, standing up a little straighter. Perhaps you might slow down when you are in conversation with another person and articulate your words more clearly. You might find yourself making more eye contact with people, listening more attentively to them when they are speaking.

Claiming yourself as a public speaker doesn't mean you are always running around giving public speeches. It simply means it's another one of the many roles you are capable of playing at various times in your life. We all have many roles we play throughout our lives whether it's a parent, friend, sibling, career person, philanthropist or whatever, the role of public speaker is just another role we sometimes engage in.

A powerful exercise is to remind yourself on a regular basis, 'I am a public speaker.' As you repeat this statement, you might find yourself remembering all the times you have spoken in public. It's a lot easier to accept a statement as fact when you have evidence to back it up. Although it's important to know (in preparation for the next section) that to claim something as true does not require evidence.

The other reason this exercise is powerful is because it helps to eliminate our own self-judgment around our ability to speak in public; a judgment we often unwittingly project onto our audience. By simply repeating, 'I am a public speaker', we remove any preconceptions we have about the kind of speaker we are. And by eliminating self-judgment, we begin the process of dissolving our fear.

Once you have claimed the role of the public speaker for yourself, you are then free to choose what kind of public speaker you wish to be. Do you want to be someone who is absolutely terrified of speaking in public or would you like to be someone who is confident, powerful and inspirational? Clearly the choice is a no-brainer.

The Big Question

Despite what you might be thinking, the type of public speaker you become is a choice. It's your choice. You can choose to be a brain-blanking, knee-clanking, teeth-chattering public speaker, or you can consciously choose to have an entirely different experience. Since I've never met anyone who wants to remain terrified while speaking on stage, I'm going to assume you are open to consciously choosing the kind of public speaker you wish to be.

So how does one choose what kind of public speaker they want to be? Well, once again, it's a surprisingly simple process. You just choose it by stating it. Let's say you want to be a world-class public speaker. You might then state: 'I choose to be a world-class public speaker'.

The reason I have people place the word 'choose' in the statement is because this word helps to bypass the rational mind, which inevitably kicks in when we state something we don't consciously believe is possible or we don't have the evidence to back it up.

If you were to state, 'I am a world-class public speaker' (which you are more than welcome to go ahead and state if that resonates with you), your rational mind is likely to jump in with a decisive, 'No, you're not!' And at this stage you're likely to agree. Your mind is likely to respond with something like, 'Yeah, you're right. I'm not a world-class public speaker. Not even close. Who the hell am I kidding?'

When you actively choose something for yourself, you begin actively moving towards it. Making a conscious decision to be a world-class public speaker (or confident, relaxed, powerful, entertaining or whatever adjective resonates with you) sets the intention in motion and you will naturally start to move towards whatever action is required for you to achieve this intention. You don't need to know how this will happen, only that it will.

There's a wonderful quote in *Alice's Adventures in Wonderland & Through the Looking Glass*, where the White Queen states, 'It's a poor sort of memory that only works backwards.' I love this quote because it reminds us that our future is not determined by our past. Instead, we have the freedom to create our present reality based on our capacity to imagine it. I can either use my past experiences to create my present or I can create new future imaginings.

Now this might sound a little far out, but this is actually based on the principles of quantum physics which have determined that time is not linear but rather a constant. All time is happening now and our present reality is based on where we choose to place our attention. In my experience, when it comes to public speaking, most people focus on past experiences, which are often negative and then use these experiences to recreate their present experience. This is not something that's done consciously. We just assume that our past must be the dictator of our future. Fortunately, this is not the case.

You only need to be able to imagine yourself as the kind of public speaker you wish to be for it to be possible. The image you construct in your mind then becomes the 'evidence' that it's possible. This is why Albert Einstein famously said, 'Imagination is more important than knowledge.' It's your imagination that creates the world you experience, not your knowledge of the world you are currently experiencing. And to quote another great man, Paul J Meyer once said, 'Whatever you vividly imagine, ardently desire, sincerely believe, and enthusiastically act upon … must inevitably come to pass!'

When I ask people what kind of speaker they want to be, the adjectives I often hear people use include: confident, powerful, present, clear, articulate, engaging, inspiring, heart-felt, informative, entertaining, among others. Never have I heard anyone say they want to become a 'perfect' public speaker. So why are we striving to become something we are not really interested in becoming? Not only is perfection an impossible standard, our audience isn't looking for us to be perfect either. Your audience just wants to see you as you are.

To find out what kind of public speaker you would like to be, just close your eyes and ask yourself, 'What kind of public speaker do I want to be?' And then wait for the answer to come. It always does.

What's your 'why'?

> *We all want to be heard, but let's acknowledge the difference between speaking up with intention and speaking up for attention.*
>
> - **Monica Lewinsky**

Why are you here? What do you want to be known for? What kind of impact do you want to have? What kind of difference do you want to make in the world? What kind of legacy do you want to leave? What knowledge, insights, wisdom, and expertise do you have to share? What gifts do you have to offer? What is your purpose for being on stage? Why are you here?

As a public speaker, these are very important questions to ask yourself, yet even more importantly is to know the answers to such questions, even if it's just for your own knowledge and awareness. Your purpose will guide you through every presentation and it will help you to stay on point so that you don't get distracted or lose your way.

The act of standing in front of a group of people who have come to listen to what we have to say is a great privilege. It's an honour to have others give us their undivided attention and it's our duty to respect it. As a public speaker, your job is to know exactly why you are there and what you have to offer otherwise we are wasting everyone's time, including our own.

When I sit down with a client one of the first things I have them do is identify their Purpose Statement. This is your reason for being on stage. It's why you are there. But it's more than just an intention or an objective of what you want to achieve, it's a statement that reflects an inner calling that is aligned with your deepest core values.

A clear Purpose Statement also helps to alleviate any negative energy associated with public speaking since the energy associated with purpose is far more powerful than nervous energy. A person who is 'on purpose' will often have the ability to overcome any obstacle in the way of achieving that purpose, especially if the purpose is aligned with their core truth.

Have you ever endured a mind-numbingly boring presentation? More than likely, it's because the speaker has not taken the time to clarify their purpose and why they are presenting, beyond the desire to meet a specific outcome or get something from the audience. Instead, they were in a state of anxiety when preparing the content and remained in that state for the duration of their presentation. Fear has a way of sucking the life and vibrancy out of creative expression, including public speaking.

I experienced this for myself while working as a television presenter in Los Angeles. Watching myself for the first time on television was like watching the talking dead. Who was this person staring back at me? My eyes were cold and blank, my body appeared frozen and paralysed. The only thing moving was my mouth and even that looked as if it were operating on automatic mode. There was nothing warm or engaging about my style. I looked and sounded like a human robot.

Knowing the absolute terror that was coursing through my veins at the time, it's no wonder this is how I came across on camera. There was no energy or life behind my words or actions; it was as if my soul had literally left my body along with all the colour of my personality. There was nothing entertaining or engaging about my presentation style, which was ironic since I was supposedly the Entertainment Reporter!

In those early days, when my public speaking style was closer to chloroform than creative expression, I would go through the motions, reciting the facts in a monotone voice as if subconsciously trying to put my audience to sleep so I wouldn't have to endure the awful possibility of humiliating myself in front of them. Over the years, as I worked on my confidence as a speaker, I found that by connecting to a purpose beyond my own need for approval and validation not only increased my confidence but helped me to take the focus off myself and keep it on my audience and how I could best be of service to them.

Purpose is cornerstone of power

Before we can identify our public speaking Purpose Statement, it's important to reclaim any power we might have unwittingly given away. So what does this actually mean?

Many people come to me because they 'have to' give a presentation even though it's something they don't really want to do. They don't feel like they have a choice and as a result believe themselves to be powerlessness around it. Now, it's very difficult to feel inspired and purposeful about something when you believe that you've been strong-armed into it.

Before I can actively help someone construct a powerful presentation, they have to know they are the ones making the choice to present. No one is forcing you to speak. This can be a challenging notion for some, especially if it is a directive coming from someone else such as a boss or as part of their role. Yet it's virtually impossible to connect to a deeper purpose when someone doesn't want to speak in the first place.

If someone is very resistant to public speaking and finds themselves in a position where they 'have' to give a speech, I will start by offering the suggestion, 'If you really don't want to present, then you don't have to. You can cancel right now.'

'But I have too,' they will say. 'I've already said I'll do it.'

'So tell them you've changed your mind.'

'I can't do that. I'll look stupid.'

'Who cares how you look?' I say. 'If you really don't want to do it, you don't have to.'

'But my boss says I have to.'

'So tell your boss you don't want to and you're not doing it.'

'But I could lose my job.'

'So you can get another one.'

'But I don't want another one.'

'So then you have a choice, don't you? You can either deliver your presentation and keep the job you want or you can not give the presentation and start looking for another job. Either way you always have a choice and it's always yours to make.'

You always have a choice when it comes to giving a presentation. Sure there might be consequences if you tell your boss or whoever you're accountable to that you're not doing it, yet this is still a choice. To accept this as your choice is to claim back any power you may have given away about public speaking. If you want to be a more powerful public speaker, then this is a good place to start.

Rachel* contacted me in this very predicament. She had an upcoming presentation that she definitely did not want to go through with. She was terrified of public speaking and felt she had been coerced into agreeing to do it. As Rachel believed she didn't have a choice she was in a state of turmoil around her presentation. When I told her to cancel the presentation, she was shocked, especially since she had come to me for help.

'But I couldn't do that,' Rachel said.

'Of course you can,' I countered. 'You just call up the client and say that you're very sorry but you're no longer available to give the presentation.'

Rachel couldn't believe what I was saying. 'Aren't you supposed to be helping me with my presentation rather than telling me to cancel it?'

'Until you recognise you have a choice in this matter, there's nothing I can do to help you. I can't give you your own power. You have to claim it for yourself and the only way you can do that, especially as a presenter, is to accept that whether or not you go through with this presentation is entirely up to you.'

Rachel had never considered she had a choice about the presentation she was scheduled to give, nor had she ever considered cancelling. She told me that she would think about it. Indeed Rachel contemplated cancelling the presentation; her anxiety levels around it were so intense. Two weeks later Rachel contacted me again and said, 'I've thought about what you said and I've decided I don't want to cancel. I want to go through with the presentation.'

'Great,' I told her. 'Now we can get to work.'

Remember, people buy why

Public speaking is not about manipulating or coercing our audience into doing something we want them to do, but it is about sharing what we have to offer knowing that it could potentially be of value. Having a clear Purpose Statement that is aligned with our core being will ensure that we can communicate effectively what we have to offer while allowing our audience to make their minds up for themselves. We can't control other people's reactions to our gift but we can ensure we've done everything in our power to make our gift as enticing and attractive as possible. We do this by having a clear understanding of why we are doing what we're doing or saying what we're saying.

Simon Sinek is a bestselling author and speaker whose TED talk has been downloaded more than twenty-two million times, which might suggest he's onto something. Simon states that, 'People don't buy what you do; they buy why you do it.' (If you haven't already seen Simon's talk, I have included a link in the Resources section at the back of the book). Knowing why you are doing something is just as important as what you are doing and how you are doing it.

When I ask people why they want to speak, often their reasons are connected to a sense of obligation rather than inspiration. They will say things like, 'Because I have to as part of my job' or, 'I have to promote my book' or, 'I have my brother's wedding coming up' or just, 'I'm going to have to do it at some point and I want to be able to speak without falling over'. While these are all valid reasons, rarely have I seen people jumping out of their boots with excitement about them.

Knowing why you are speaking is just as important, if not more so, than what you are actually saying. Sometimes I will spend an entire session with someone just getting clear on their public speaking Purpose Statement. Why are they speaking? Why do they feel this is important? Why do they believe this? Why? Why? Why? If the answer isn't exciting them, then chances are they are not going to feel excited about speaking. And if they are not excited about what they are saying, chances are their audience isn't going to be excited either.

Before you do anything in relation to your presentation, take the time to craft your public speaking Purpose Statement. Make sure it's a statement that generates a positive feeling in your body and once you've achieved this, repeat it regularly until it becomes a part of your being. Remember, this is not something you have to share with others. Your Purpose Statement is just for you even though it will end up serving those you end up presenting to.

Crafting your Purpose Statement

Now that you have made the choice to present, it's time to connect to your purpose for doing so. If there is anything you take away from this book, let it be this: your purpose will define your presentation. It will shape what you say and how you say it. It will provide not only the foundation for your experience on stage, but for your audience as well. Before you begin preparing anything, make sure you sit down and contemplate why you are there in the first place. And make sure it's something that *brings you to life*.

Judy* contacted me because she had been asked to deliver a keynote to a group of female creative directors and had agreed to do it on the basis that it would be great exposure for her business. Judy was a highly accomplished and confident woman and instead of being afraid at the prospect at public speaking, she was looking forward to the opportunity. Having never delivered a keynote presentation before, Judy wanted some guidance on how to create a keynote and structure her ideas. When she came to me she had her content well-prepared and flipped open her laptop with an expectation that we would get straight into structuring her ideas.

'Before we get into the content, first tell me why you want to speak in public?' I asked her.

'Well, it's a great opportunity to promote my business,' she replied (too easy!).

'Okay, great,' I said. 'Why do you want to do that?'

Judy laughed as if to say, 'Well, isn't that obvious?' She replied, 'Well, because I'm good at what I do and by speaking in public I can help more people.'

'Excellent. That's a great reason. Why do you want to help people?'

At this point Judy was starting to look a little annoyed. I could tell she was wondering why I was asking her so many questions and when we were going to start working on her presentation.

'Okay, so I want to help people because I know that what I do improves people's lives.'

We were starting to get somewhere. What Judy didn't know was that, rather than listening to the words she was saying, I was listening instead to the non-verbal information she was giving me and up to this point everything about her body language told me that her reasons for giving this presentation were about being responsible and fulfilling her obligation as a businesswoman. There was little-to-no excitement in her voice or body language and presentations devoid of emotion inevitably lack inspiration or memorability. And so I continued the line of questioning.

'So why do you want to improve people's lives?'

Judy took a deep breath in, as if starting to feel irritated. She took a moment to think about the question before eventually replying, 'Because I love seeing people change their lives for the better.'

Now we were really getting somewhere. When Judy said the word 'love' I noticed a spark in her eyes. Something lit up inside her that told me we were on the right track. Yet while I could tell that Judy really did love what she did, it still didn't answer why she wanted to speak in public.

'So why do you want to make people lives better?' I asked again.

This is the point where Judy drew a blank. This is always a good sign. When people draw a blank it's always a sign that the answer is close. Very close. In Judy's case, the block was that she believed it was selfish to get something out of helping others. She felt it was wrong to feel good about being of service to other people.

After some gentle prodding eventually Judy admitted, 'When I know I'm helping someone, it feels amazing. It's incredible. It feels like I'm living my purpose and I'm doing what I'm here to do. I feel like I'm fulfilling my mission in life.'

Boom! And there it was. When Judy said this, her whole demeanour changed. She relaxed back in her chair, a smile stretched out across her face and her eyes shone. Suddenly all the tension and the irritation melted away and she began laughing.

'Ahhhhh, I see what you're doing,' she said.

I laughed along with her. 'So let me ask you again,' I said. 'Tell me why you're speaking?'

She smiled and said, 'The reason I want to speak is because by doing so I will be living my purpose and fulfilling my mission in life. But not only that, I want to challenge myself in new ways. I want to better myself and public speaking is something I've always wanted to do.'

'Great! How does that feel when you say that?'

'Amazing. Incredible. I can't wait to get up on stage.'

As I looked across the table at Judy it was like looking at a different woman to the one who had first walked through the door. Judy was beaming and the lift in energy in the room was palpable. Now we were ready to work on her presentation.

So let's get real

So now that we have addressed what public speaking really is about and our true purpose for engaging in such an act, there is no excuse to avoid an opportunity to speak in public should it arise (and it will) or deliver a mind-blowingly boring and lack-lustre presentation ever again. Sure we might still be experiencing some anxiety around the idea of having to present in public but that's to be expected and we will address this in the following step. But for now, let's agree that we will never deliver another boring presentation ever again. And just to be sure, please repeat after me:

I promise never to deliver a boring presentation ever again.

Great. Now that we've got that out of the way we can get on with why we are here and that's to learn how to deliver a more engaging and creative presentation.

Knowing only too well how mortifying and terrifying the experience of public speaking can be, I'm enormously grateful that today I can stand up in front of people and actually speak in coherent sentences, with a smile on my face and a spring in my step. It's an amazing feeling. These days, rather than something to fear, I see the opportunity to speak to an audience as a privilege. My job is to make their experience a worthwhile one. When you're able to enjoy yourself, your audience does as well.

It's important to remember, you always have a choice. You can make public speaking about yourself or we can make it about others. One way leads directly to the offices of public speaking coaches such as myself, and one way leads to enjoyment and fun and the knowledge that we are making a difference in the world in our own unique way. Which would you choose? (Now, from an economic perspective I do require a small percentage of you to choose the first option, in which case my contact details are at the back of this book.)

Of course my hope is that you decide to see public speaking as an opportunity to be of service to others. I assure you that by doing so you will open up to the possibility of public speaking being one of the most rewarding, joyful and memorable experiences you will ever have.

Key 2
Prepare to Be Yourself

Our deepest fear is not that we are inadequate. Our deepest fear is that we are powerful beyond measure. It is our light, not our darkness that most frightens us. We ask ourselves, 'Who am I to be brilliant, gorgeous, talented, fabulous?' Actually, who are you not to be? You are a child of God. Your playing small does not serve the world. There is nothing enlightened about shrinking so that other people won't feel insecure around you. We are all meant to shine, as children do. We were born to make manifest the glory of God that is within us. It's not just in some of us; it's in everyone. And as we let our own light shine, we unconsciously give other people permission to do the same. As we are liberated from our own fear, our presence automatically liberates others.

MARIANNE WILLIAMSON, *A Return To Love*

I always think of my presentations as a growth process that I'm continuously going through.

DR WAYNE W DYER, *I AM VIDEO SERIES*

One morning while on a break during one of my work-shops, I was wandering through the city in search of some lunch when I received a phone call from an events manager called Linda*. Linda was organising a lunch for one hundred or so accountants and, having read a column I had written in a magazine, thought I would be the perfect person to speak at her upcoming event.

'I was wondering if you would be available to be our key-note speaker?' she asked.

'Sure,' I told her, excitedly. 'I would love to speak at your event.'

While I hadn't actually delivered a keynote presentation before, I had been running presentation skills workshops for corporate clients for a couple of years. The days of crumbling in front of cameras were far behind me and my confidence had grown exponentially. I was thrilled about Linda's opportunity as it would give me a chance to put my teachings into practice and 'walk my talk'.

Even though the event was almost six months out, I imme-diately began ruminating on what I would say, allowing the ideas and thoughts to swirl around in my head. As the months rolled on, I began putting my ideas onto paper and slowly began crafting my keynote. Yet as the event drew closer, I noticed my tension levels rising.

I continuing making more notes, created more slides and began pacing up and down hallways while mumbling to myself in an effort to ease my anxiety. As the days ticked over, my apprehension grew until a couple of months out from the event I really started to panic.

What the hell am I doing? This is crazy! I'm going to bomb. I can't do this. How can I get out of this?

My nerves about delivering a keynote presentation to a hundred people had turned into complete terror. I felt trapped, restricted, out of control. I was not only out of my depth; I was out of my mind. I had to figure out some way to get out of it. But how?

When Linda called a month before the event to touch base and confirm the details, there was only one thing I could do: I was going to have to lie.

'I'm really sorry,' I said. 'I'm afraid I'm not going to be able to give the presentation as I've just been called to make an emergency trip to New Zealand. Unfortunately I'm going to be there on the day of the presentation.'

There was silence on the end of the line. My heart was racing. Of course there was no emergency and there was no scheduled trip to New Zealand, but I figured it would be safer to say I was out of the country, ensuring there would no way I could be cajoled into speaking at the upcoming lunch. I felt terrible for lying but not as terrible as I had been feeling for the past month. In fact, knowing that I no longer had to present meant I felt better than I had in a long time.

'That's a real shame,' said Linda eventually. 'We've sent out the invitations and we've already started to receive RSVPs.'

'I'm really sorry,' I told her, despite feeling more relieved than sorry.

'Well, I guess we don't have any other choice,' she said. 'When are you back from New Zealand?'

'Oh, um … what do you mean?' I asked, unprepared for the question. Since I wasn't actually going to New Zealand, I hadn't thought to schedule my fake return date.

'When are you back from New Zealand?'

'The following week,' I said hesitantly.

'Okay then,' she said with a sigh. 'We will just have to postpone the event until the following week. I'll change the invitations and send them back out. I'm sure it won't be too much of a problem.'

'Oh…wonderful,' I said while shaking my head in despair. There was nothing more I could do. I was going to have to go through with the presentation, just after my fake holiday to New Zealand.

As it turned out, the presentation went relatively well and the feedback I received was extremely positive, both from the audience and from Linda. Although I knew that if I was going to be a professional public speaker (rather than just a facilitator of public speaking skills), I was going to have to get over this fear that was still plaguing me. It wasn't enough to just come up with a bunch of strategies and techniques in the hope of countering any anxiety I might find myself experiencing. To be the kind of public speaker I truly wanted to be and knew I was capable of being meant diving directly into the heart of this fear and transforming it once and for all. This is what it means to prepare to be yourself.

We are born original

One of my favourite pastimes is people watching and it's why I often arrive early at an airport, or can spend hours wandering aimlessly around a new city. I love the opportunity to silently observe the passers-by and contemplate the stories they carry along with them.

During a trip to Los Angeles several years ago, I had a profound realisation while watching the passing parade from a little café in the middle of 3rd Street Promenade in Santa Monica. With a few hours before I was due to catch my flight home, I stopped for a bite to eat, choosing a table where I would be in full view of the crowded marketplace.

Not long after I sat down, I became aware of a high-pitched bell ringing nearby and turned around to see a young, well-dressed African American man in a knee-length cashmere coat and scarf, leaning against the railing with the offending bell in hand. He was standing next to an empty Red Cross bucket, looking bored as hundreds of people strode past. No one paid any attention to him, the bell or the empty bucket.

As I watched the man listlessly ringing his bell, I began wondering about his life. How did he come to be working for the Red Cross? How come he was so well dressed? Where did he live? How old was he? He looked young and I wondered whether he was going to college or working. Where were his parents? Did he have a girlfriend? Was he born in Los Angeles or did he move here? If so, where from? What were his interests and passions? (It certainly wasn't fund-raising!) Had he experienced tragedy? If so, what? Who were his role models? What made him laugh?

The man, oblivious to my private musings on his life's details, carried on ringing his bell and for a moment I had the strange experience of feeling so close to this person even though I knew nothing about him, and he didn't even know I existed. While I didn't know the answers to my questions about his life, I knew there were answers and somewhere within them I was certain I would find some common links. I didn't know what hardships he might have faced in his life, but I was certain he must have experienced some, as we all have. Knowing this made me feel connected to this man.

My attention then shifted to the people walking past him. They were also lost in worlds of their own. I speculated about these worlds as well. Some people strode with urgency and direction. I wondered where they were going. Back to work? Or home? Where did they work? What did they do? Did they enjoy it? Where did they live? Who did they live with? Were they happy? If not, why not?

Of all the people who passed by, not one was like another. I noticed they were of all of different colours, shapes and sizes. Some hurried while others strolled. Some chatted and laughed with friends while others walked alone expressionless, with headphones attached to their ears. One couple, appearing lost, kept turning around in circles while craning their necks towards the tops of the buildings. A policeman trailed slowly behind a woman in a pink leotard with a fur jacket slung over one shoulder, who was having an animated conversation with the air. Three women in skin-tight jeans, knee-high boots and swinging Victoria's Secret bags strutted down the promenade as if on a catwalk, pouting as if there were hidden paparazzi in the crowd.

Through the haze of everyday ordinariness, I became aware of the extraordinariness of every single person. While the minute details eluded me, I sensed the inner worlds of each, experiencing the common links between us all. As they walked past, I could sense the stories they carried within them. Underneath the clothes and behind the masks were their ideas and eccentricities; their heartbreaks and callings and fears. I experienced the differences and the sameness of each person all at once and in that moment my entire being felt open and expanded. It was as if in that moment I was experiencing the extraordinariness of each person, including myself.

My thoughts then turned to the billions of other souls wandering along other promenades, shopping for lingerie or talking to imaginary friends, all containing the same extraordinariness within their everyday ordinariness. By the time I finished my sandwich, I was completed blissed out, feeling a sense of connection to everyone and in awe of this infinitely intelligent universe that has the power to create such unique magnificence so many times over. It was truly the best sandwich I've ever had!

Original gifts

We are all walking expressions of this infinite universal intelligence. As you are reading this now, your heart is beating on its own, your lungs are inhaling life-sustaining air, your cells are recycling and replenishing themselves, your stomach is digesting food, your hair and fingernails are growing, and your brain is processing the millions of bits of information passing by your eyes, including these words. We are literally walking and talking miracles, so awesome and incredible it's no wonder we wander around malls and promenades, acting as if nothing miraculous is happening. It's simply too much to contemplate.

Along with this extraordinary capability to sustain our own lives without a single conscious thought, we come into this world bringing with us gifts to share with others. These gifts are unique to us and whether we are aware of our gifts or not, we all have them. Our gifts live within us and carry the desire to be expressed through us. You will have a pretty good idea of what your gift is by the way you feel when you are engaged with it.

Joy is the most obvious marker. If you experience a sense of joy when engaged in an activity, then that's a good sign it's one of your gifts that is calling to be expressed through you. Other symptoms include losing track of time, forgetting where you are and being overwhelmed with a sense of pleasure and contentment. It could be gardening, cooking, surfing, writing, painting, acting, creating budgets, dancing, teaching, rock climbing, train spotting, woodworking, flower arranging, fishing, computer programming, or any other such endeavour. It literally doesn't matter what it is, just as long as it matters to you.

While we all have gifts that are unique to us, strangely public speaking isn't often one of them. It's not often you come across someone who experiences an overwhelming sense of joy and pleasure and contentment at the prospect of speaking in front of an audience. Of course such people do exist but they're probably not the ones reading a book like this, so I'm going to assume that you're not one of them. And I'm certainly not either.

One of the gifts I brought with me into this life is writing. I know this simply from the sheer joy I experience every time I sit down with my notebook and pen or at my computer. It's got nothing to do with how well (or not well) I can write. It's the action of writing that matters. I can be writing complete crap and still be in a state of joy simply because I'm engaged in the process.

When I'm writing, literally hours will go by before I've realised I've been lost within whatever world is being created on the page. Writing is also perhaps the only time where I feel completely at peace within myself and at ease with life. When I'm writing, everything somehow has a way of being okay, even if it's not.

Public speaking, on the other hand, has been a very different experience. While I'm absolutely passionate about self-expression and I love both public speaking and writing as vehicles for this, if I had to choose between the two I would always opt for the quiet safety of my notebook. Whereas writing was always something that came naturally to me, public speaking has been one long arm wrestle.

Yet just because public speaking may not come naturally to me as it might to some, doesn't mean that it's something to turn away from. Even though public speaking may not be that thing that lights us up and puts a smile on our faces, doesn't make it any less of a worthy pursuit. Rather than being my gift, public speaking has actually been a gift to me. It's enabled me to get to know and appreciate myself in ways I could not have otherwise done. I see public speaking as an opportunity to share my gifts with the world, rather than being my gift in the world.

Our gifts are everything that make us inherently unique, something that we all are. These include our stories, personal experiences, insights, knowledge and wisdom. There is no one on this planet who has lived the life that you have lived or had the experiences that you have had. Your life is one of a kind. It's perfectly original and unique.

Have you ever noticed when telling a story that suddenly the energy in the room shifts? People sit up a little straighter, they lean in a little more closely, listen a little harder. We all want to know what the view is like from everyone else's window. Yet as we can only see the view from our own window, we must rely on others to share their view with us.

Nowadays, I approach the opportunity to present with a curious excitement rather than a sense of dread or panic. Not only am I sharing my gifts with others, it's an experience that will always teach me something new about myself. While I'm passionate about being of service, I'm just as passionate about self-examination and inquiry. There's always more to learn.

And there is no place more perfect to do that than on a stage in front of hundreds of people.

'Be yourself, everyone else is taken'

Oscar Wilde was truly on to something when he said this. One of my all-time favourite quotes, I remember the shock I felt the first time I heard it. *What a concept!* I thought, having realised that I had spent much of my life trying to be what other people wanted or expected me to be, despite no one actually wanting or expecting anything from me. It was all in my head anyway.

Most of us are wandering around with Public and Private versions of ourselves. If you don't believe me then just spend a few minutes on Instagram or Facebook. Our public version is the version we present to the world based on what we think others want to see or what we believe will attract validation and approval and applause. We have this idea that in order to be accepted by others we must conceal the parts we believe are 'ugly' or unacceptable. Now, there's nothing bad or wrong about doing this, it's just a natural stage of development.

I remember turning up at pre-school for the first time as a little girl, and suddenly becoming aware of all the ways I was different from others. Most notable was my height. I was well and truly head and shoulders above every other kid in the playground, something that I soon discovered was not a favourable trait as it instantly separated me from others. Unfortunately there wasn't much I could do about this so I tried to make myself smaller in other ways.

I quickly learned that it wasn't safe to bring any kind of attention to myself if I could possibly avoid it. For example, during one particular day at kindergarten I wanted to show off my brand new orange swimsuit, which I'd decided to wear under my dress. While playing in the playground I whipped off my dress and began prancing around in my new swimsuit. A teacher spotted me and from across the crowded playground shouted, 'Hedley, put your clothes back on and stop showing off. You look ridiculous!'

The teacher's words stung, especially because the other kids stopped to see what all the commotion was about. I ran inside burning with humiliation as my spirit began acclimatizing to this sometimes-cruel new world. I came to the conclusion, as many of us do during these early years, that it wasn't safe to be myself – rather it was better to hide in the crowd and avoid being noticed at all costs. And so Public Hedley and Private Hedley were born.

Unfortunately we can't hide forever and life has a way of creating situations to bring us back out of our self-constructed shells that have been carefully shaped and polished over our lifetimes. Public speaking is one of these ways. When we are standing alone in front of an audience of people, there is simply nowhere to hide. We can either resist the experience by fearing it and avoiding or we can surrender to it fully and trust that, regardless of our fears, everything will be okay. We will be okay.

This can be difficult, especially if we've experienced situations in the past where we learned it wasn't okay to be ourselves or to express ourselves. One of the gifts public speaking has to offer is this reconnection with our true self and the honest expression of this self. This is not an overnight process. It's often a slow and ongoing process that requires patience and diligence.

Public speaking is a wonderful way of learning how to connect even more deeply with our true essence. My fear of public speaking propelled me into this career which I'm absolutely passionate about. By helping others to transform their fears, I continue to transform my own. These days I feel more myself when I'm on stage in front of an audience than I ever thought was possible. It's one of the most liberating and fulfilling experiences I believe you can have. And it's one I definitely recommend for everyone.

There is no comparison

One of the things people do when attempting to improve their public speaking skills is look to other world-class speakers who are demonstrating the principles they wish to possess. People will attempt to emulate Barack Obama or Oprah Winfrey or a whole host of other masterful speakers as if this is the answer to their public speaking challenges. Not only have I seen many people in my workshops attempt this impossible feat, I too have attempted it.

I remember seeing Jessica Rowe speak at a conference in Sydney a number of years ago and I was so impressed by the way she spoke, her immaculate style, and the way she held herself on stage, I thought to myself, *I'd like to have a stage presence like her.* She had such a natural ease on stage and I thought she was the perfect speaker.

A few months later I was asked to host an event and my thoughts turned to Jessica. I decided to emulate her poise and confidence and I even bought a dress with her style in mind. Not surprisingly, while the event went well, I found I couldn't relax completely. The whole time I was on stage, I didn't feel myself. Interestingly, after the event someone came up to me and said I reminded them of Jessica Rowe!

It's wonderful to appreciate the brilliance of others but it's another thing to study them in an effort to become like them. In our attempt to be like others, we fail to be ourselves, not realising that we too possess our greatness and grandness if we would only just take a moment to recognise it within ourselves.

Public speaking is an opportunity to share our unique view of the world with others. When we approach public speaking in this way, there is no comparison. For who is there to compare with if there is only one of you? Original isn't something that we can aspire to be. We are the expression of originality. All we are doing when we stand up to speak in front of an audience is expressing this.

Public speaking isn't a skill to acquire. Rather, it's an opportunity to peel back the layers of the shell we have moulded around ourselves as self-protection. Speaking in public isn't something more we have to learn. Instead, it's a process of unlearning. There's nothing we need to do in order to be ourselves. To be an effective public speaker requires only knowing this at an experiential level.

The truth is public speaking is not the cause of our fear. Despite the common perception, public speaking is not what people are most afraid of. What we are really afraid of is discovering that we are not who we thought ourselves to be. Of course we are far greater than our own limited minds can imagine. Yet for a human being, to face uncertainty in life is to face the certainty of death. And that's not exactly everyone's idea of a good time!

Your relationship with fear

> *A life lived in fear is a life half lived.*
> **- From the movie, Strictly Ballroom**

If we are going to face our fears we should first change the way we approach fear and its presence our lives. When writing about our innate resistance to fear, *The War of Art: Winning the Inner Creative Battle* author, Steven Pressfield, uses an example from the television program, *Inside The Actors Studio*, with James Lipton. One of the questions Lipton often asks his famous guests are the factors that draw them to the roles they take on.

During an interview with George Clooney, Lipton asked what drew him to accept the role of Matt King in *The Descendants.*

Clooney responded: 'When you're looking at what you're trying to do as an actor, particularly the older you get, you're constantly trying to push into things that make you uncomfortable. I had played a character called Michael Clayton in *Up In The Air* who was a guy in control only to realise that he had no control. Matt King is a character that has never had control. He loses every argument to a ten year old. He can't win anything and has to learn, not just to forgive all the problems that have come to him that aren't his fault, he has to learn to forgive himself along the way. I thought that these were all such interesting character pieces that I couldn't have done, as an actor, five years ago. I enjoyed the fact that I was allowed to dip my toe into an area that I'm very uncomfortable in. It's exciting, it makes you nervous.'

Yes, George Clooney is human and he experiences fear, even after all the success he's achieved in his career. Although, perhaps the reason he has achieved so much is because of his relationship with his fear. Clooney appears to use fear as a tool to assist him to navigate through the many opportunities that come his way. Instead of running for the hills when a challenging project arises, Clooney perceives the existence of fear as something exciting and to be further explored. His concerns about whether he could pull off a character such as Matt King in *The Descendants* was like an internal beacon going off, calling him towards it. Rather than turn his back on the role, accepting that he wouldn't be able to pull it off, he went for it, and relished the opportunity.

Fear is a necessary part of life. It keeps us alive and out of the way of incoming traffic. Although what can sometimes happen is that we lose the ability to discern the difference between the fear that is serving us and the fear that is holding us back.

I remember participating in a course many years ago where we were asked to write down everything we were afraid of. Once I got started, my pen just kept moving. My list went on for pages and it quickly became apparent that I was afraid of a lot more than just snakes and spiders. I was afraid of *life!* This was a great exercise for me to do as it forced me to recognise my fears before deciding how I was going to move forward in my life, knowing that I didn't want to spend the rest of my days in a constant state of fear.

One of the reasons I've come to love public speaking is that it's provided a context through which my fears have been illuminated, along with a platform through which I'm able to heal and transcend them.

Yes, public speaking is about being of service to others, but it's also a way for us to be of service to ourselves in the sense we are able to reject everything that is no longer serving us, including our fear. Rather than being afraid of public speaking, the presence of this fear is an invitation to take a closer look at what it might be trying to tell us or teach us about ourselves. Our fear is an opportunity to, like Clooney, see it as something exciting, despite the discomfort we might be feeling, and move towards it knowing that we are bound to discover something that we might not have otherwise discovered.

When fear isn't really fear

> *Henry Fonda was still throwing up before each
> stage performance, even when he was seventy-
> five. In other words, fear doesn't go away.*
> - **Steven Pressfield, The War of Art**

From the first moment I experienced that leg-wobbling,
hand-shaking, brain-freezing fear in front of the television
camera, I've been fascinated with understanding everything
there is to know about the fear of public speaking. I've also
long wondered why this so-called fear of public speaking never
seems to completely go away, even after reading all the books
and doing all the courses. It seems that for many of us we have
simply accepted that public speaking is something that induces
fear and there is absolutely nothing we can do about it, other
than implement a few tricks and strategies.

Whenever I questioned where this fear originated and why
it continued to be so persistent, I was always given the same
theory: human beings are pack animals and as long as we are
stepping outside the pack we will always experience the fear
of being eaten alive. Okay, so I can accept that our brains go
into 'fight or flight' response when faced with an unknown
and threatening situation. And yet this doesn't explain why
we continue experiencing fear when faced with the prospect of
public speaking. After we've stood up in front of a roomful of
people a few times, it's no longer an 'unknown' situation. We
also quickly come to understand that public speaking is not a
threatening situation either. There is simply no genuine threat

to our lives when we stand up to speak, despite our continuing belief that there is.

This 'herd' theory, along with many of the other theories I've heard over the years, simply fails to explain not only why so many of us experience a fear of public speaking, but also why we continue to experience this fear. It simply doesn't make sense.

What then is really going on?

After years of participating in public speaking skills courses, facilitating such courses, coaching clients, writing two books on the topic and continuing to speak regularly in public, I've come to realise that the fear of public speaking isn't actually fear. At least it's not in the way we've believed it to be. This so-called anxiety we experience at the prospect of having to speak in public isn't actually fear … rather it's shame.

Allow me to explain.

When I ask people to tell me exactly what they are afraid of when it comes to public speaking, most will struggle to come up with a clear answer. Their fear is real; at least that's how it feels, but they haven't taken the time to clarify exactly what they are afraid of. When I point out that there is literally no genuine threat to their lives when speaking in public, I will ask the question again, 'So exactly what are you afraid of?'

This is where I will hear a variety of answers:

- They won't like me
- I'll fuck it up
- People will judge me
- I'm too fat/tall/short/thin/ugly
- I feel like a fraud
- I'm not qualified/credible/intelligent enough

And so on.

The experience of fear regarding public speaking is therefore not so much related to a genuine threat to life but rather a genuine threat to being exposed. In other words, it's not fear we're experiencing, at least not fear in the true sense, instead what we are really experiencing is *shame.*

By differentiating between fear and shame, we can better understand our experience of public speaking and thereby transform it. Otherwise, it would be like going to the doctor with a skin rash and being treated for a stomach ache. Before you can appropriately treat something, you first have to identify the *real* issue. When it comes to treating the fear of public speaking, we must address the *cause* of the fear rather than just the symptoms. And in my opinion, based on much examination and experimentation, the cause of the fear of public speaking is shame.

Shame

Shame is a *learned* state of being, founded on a *learned* belief that who we are is not okay. Such a belief often stems from the result of an event we experienced as children when our capacity to rationalise such an event was limited. It could be something as significant as abuse or seemingly insignificant as wearing an orange swimming suit to school and being told by a teacher to go and put some clothes on. Whatever it might be, we've all experienced such moments that left us with the impression that somehow we were wrong while not possessing the ability to fully appreciate why.

As children we were unable to understand why we were singled out, ignored or made fun of, or why our needs were not met in the specific moment we needed them to be. Since we are in an egocentric phase of development as children, when we *do* something wrong we don't have the capacity to separate our identity from our behaviour and we make the assumption that we must *be* wrong. We believe 'I am wrong' rather than 'my behaviour is wrong'. Shame is the resulting experience of this 'I am wrong' assumption.

Seemingly insignificant childhood events can therefore turn into extremely significant events, especially since it's these events that help form our early beliefs about ourselves and the world we exist in. These beliefs then serve to drive and direct our decision-making and subsequent behaviour well into adulthood. And unless we take a moment to stop and challenge these beliefs as adults, we risk spending our entire lives driven by ideas that were formed when we were not long out of nappies.

In my case, the events in my past experience such as the one in the playground and while reading out the prayer at the school assembly, along with many other experiences, left me believing that I must be wrong in some way. This resulted in feeling ashamed of who I was. I learned that to express myself in front of others means risking public humiliation. This led to the awful feeling of shame. It's no surprise I started to become more shy and introverted as I began to grow up.

What we don't realise is that most of us are harbouring feelings of personal shame. As we develop from children into teenagers and later into adults, it becomes easier to push those uncomfortable experiences away, burying them in what ultimately becomes our subconscious mind. And while it might be possible to move through life effectively without too much angst, it only takes the experience of being asked to speak in public for that shame and terror to rise up once more.

In that instant we become like eight years olds all over again. Suddenly we feel the fear of being humiliated and we instantly want to run. Our hearts start racing, palms start sweating and knees start knocking despite now being a rational, functional adult capable of completing a whole manner of complex tasks. We believe what we are feeling is fear because it certainly feels a lot like it. Yet with no genuine threat to our lives, it's not fear we are experiencing it's shame masquerading as fear, shame that was formed from a very long time ago and which has been long forgotten. Until now.

Acknowledging the one in 'fear'

Imagine a child has just come to you and told you they have a stomach ache. Would you tell that child to stop being ridiculous and just get over it? Hopefully not. If the child is experiencing a genuine anxiety about something, you would most likely support them in whatever way is appropriate until the discomfort passes. You would sit with them and listen to them, perhaps offer some words of understanding and support. In other words, you would *love* them.

This is exactly how we must begin to treat ourselves when it comes to dealing with our shame that may have been triggered through the act of public speaking. This is why a 'fear' of public speaking can be a kind of gift because it offers the opportunity to develop a more loving connection with the part of ourselves that still feels ashamed. After all, that part of ourselves is a much younger version of whom we are today, since shame is often a result of an experience we were not able to appropriately understand at the time.

While our childhood experiences help shape our characters and personalities, we are unable to understand why Mummy or Daddy are not there when we needed them; we don't know why the other kids laugh at us during Show & Tell or why they ignore us in the playground. Instead we are left to make assumptions that lead to beliefs that eventually lead to this shame. Some of the more common and universal shame-inducing beliefs are:

- I'm wrong
- I'm not good enough
- The world is not safe
- I can't trust anyone
- It's not okay to be myself

Can you relate to any of these? I know I can. Part of preparing to be yourself is to start acknowledging this younger part of ourselves that still harbours these beliefs and feelings. As we have become adults, the further away and more disconnected from this younger self we've become. What we might not be consciously aware of is that we are still reacting from these childhood wounds and beliefs in our current situations, such as having to deliver a presentation.

Acknowledging our child self and forging a relationship with this aspect of ourselves is the beginning of becoming a whole person. Until we acknowledge and integrate this part of ourselves, we will continue to facilitate a false persona to the external world, keeping those shameful aspects hidden and out of sight. Doing this only fosters the fear that, at some point, we will be exposed and found out.

Continuing to ignore this younger, wounded aspect of ourselves is what leads to self-sabotage in high stakes situations such as public speaking. I see this often in my workshops and coaching sessions. Someone might be the most capable, confident and functional person in all other areas of their life but the moment they step on stage in front of an audience, they crumble. The child self has taken over and will do anything to avoid being exposed or humiliated.

When we don't acknowledge and give space to our shame, we continue to avoid or suppress it while it continues to maintain power over us. I've seen perfectly healthy, intelligent, functional adults react to public speaking in a whole manner of ways from calling in sick, taking pills, having panic attacks, throwing up or even planning fake holidays to New Zealand as a way of getting out of having to give a presentation! Until we acknowledge our shame we will continue to act out in all sort of irrational ways, like a child who will do anything to get out of something it desperately doesn't want to do.

The only way to dealing with our fear of public speaking is to acknowledge the shame existing within. Shame is not a pleasant experience which is why we spend so much of our life turning away from it. Yet the moment we turn to face, acknowledge and allow it to exist, shame loses its power and potency. Shame, disguised as fear, no longer runs the show.

Just Be (with) Yourself

> *To be yourself is to be with yourself.*
>
> - **Matt Kahn**

'Just be yourself.' These are common words of advice people give those about to embark on the daunting task of speaking in public, especially those shaking in their boots at the prospect. It's a sage piece of advice, if only we knew what it meant. So, what does it actually mean to be yourself?

Spiritual teacher Matt Kahn says, 'To be yourself is the ability to be *with* yourself.' This means to be present with whatever experience is arising in each moment. I love this definition because it's a simple reminder to just be with whatever experience is arising in the moment, regardless of whether we judge it as comfortable or uncomfortable. Presence is one of the greatest gifts we can give ourselves as well as others. Once we are capable of being present with ourselves then we can be present with others. Our capacity to be present is what gives us our *presence*.

Public speaking is a whole body experience – as much a physical activity as a mental and emotional one. Although in my experience, to truly show up as yourself for others as a public speaker also requires the engagement of your spiritual side.

And since we are engaging our whole being – this phenomenally intelligent, self-regulating, intuitive, beautiful instrument – when we speak, it's therefore incredibly important we have a close and connected relationship with our entire being, including body, mind and spirit.

Loving the skin you're in

When we stand up to speak, we do so dressed in our physical body. Every single body is perfectly unique and different to the next. It's another stamp of originality. Yet it's also the cause for the most self-judgment and criticism, and therefore fear and shame. If we are going to be inspirational public speakers then it's important we have a healthy relationship with our physical body first.

While there is much to admire about our beautiful and brilliant bodies, the research will tell us that over 97 per cent of women will have at least one negative thought about their body every single day. I suspect the statistics are similar for men. The fashion and beauty industry is built on and invested in our continuous self-hatred of and the constant need to improve our physical appearance. As a society we've become accustomed to chopping, changing, inserting, removing, shaving and smoothing anything that doesn't fit our perceived mould of 'perfect'. 'Body shaming' has become so widespread and prevalent, it's no wonder so many people would rather hide in a dark corner rather than stand up on stage under a spotlight.

I know only too well about this. Being a woman standing at six foot one-and-a-half inches (186cm), I have had my fair share of physical insecurities. While I have a healthy relationship with my body these days, this hasn't always been the case. At fourteen years of age I was already pushing six feet. I was more than a head taller than everyone else. When all you want as a teenager is to fit in, this was literally impossible for me. Naturally, I blamed my parents.

My parents did try to address the problem of a rapidly rising child. They took me to a doctor. The doctor kindly x-rayed my wrist bone and predicted that my growth spurt would continue for another couple of inches before eventually stopping somewhere around the six foot one-and-a-half mark. Receiving this news was like being told I only had a month to live, which in that moment, I would have preferred.

Immediately I began researching possible solutions to my unacceptable dilemma and discovered an operation that was only performed in Japan (the only place it was legal) that could make people taller. Now, I certainly didn't want to be taller, but I figured if doctors could insert fake shinbones into short Japanese legs to make them longer, surely they could take a few inches out of mine? I pitched the idea to my parents. Not surprisingly, they refused.

Mum did want to help though. After doing some of her own research she came up with another, more practical solution: a support group for tall people called … wait for it … SKYSCRAPERS.

As if being tall wasn't bad enough, now my mother wanted me to join a club where I would be surrounded by other tall people. Sure, I would travel halfway around the world to have some bone chopped out of my legs, but attend a support group for tall people called Skyscrapers? Naturally, I didn't respond to her suggestion very well.

However, despite my endless protesting, my mother booked me in for the next 'get-together' which was a luncheon in Vaucluse, a wealthy suburb in Sydney where many of the city's rich – and apparently tall – people lived. The cost of entry was less financial and more incremental. You had to be at least six feet tall, which put me in an unusual predicament – I was too short!

To my surprise, I didn't hate the lunch although I did struggle a little walking in a pair of heels for the first time. As it turned out, I wasn't the only tall girl in Sydney. There were others just like me. Some even taller, which left me feeling strangely grateful. Yet possibly the best part about the lunch was that for the first time in my life, I got to experience what it was like to literally 'fit in'. And while the experience didn't cure my wish to be shorter, it helped knowing I wasn't alone in my 'tall-comings'.

Learning to love one's body regardless of its size or shape or appearance is essential to being present as a public speaker. You can't be present with your audience if you're not in your body or wishing you had someone else's. Body shame is one of the most common reasons why people are terrified of public speaking and attempt to hide behind aids such as PowerPoint or a lectern. When we are uncomfortable in our own skin, it's almost impossible to stand calmly and confidently in front of a spotlight and maintain our composure with a hundred pairs of eyes staring at us. It can be a very scary and intimidating place to be. Our physical insecurities drive many of our fears about speaking in public because we are afraid people will recognise our perceived flaws and judge us on that basis. It's therefore important we come to love our physical bodies.

Your body is your instrument

It wasn't until many years after my 'Skyscraper' experience that I really started to accept my physicality although it wasn't until I had an unexpected meeting with a mirror that I really came to perceive my body with a new perspective.

While catching up with a friend in a bar I excused myself to go to the bathroom which turned out to be incredibly difficult to find due to the floor to ceiling mirrors, the dim lighting and the several cocktails I'd already consumed. Walking down a hallway, I noticed a very tall woman coming towards me. *Wow, she's tall*, I thought. It very quickly and painfully became evident that the 'very tall woman' was me and instead of walking into the bathroom I had walked into a mirror.

It was an incredibly surreal and insightful experience. While it only lasted a few seconds, in those seconds I had the experience of what it was like to view myself from outside myself. While I noticed that 'the woman' was tall, very tall in fact, I noticed that there was no judgment around this fact. It wasn't positive or negative. It was simply a fact. Having always entertained the belief that my height was a negative and something that other people viewed as negative, this was an extraordinarily liberating insight.

By realising that people are not necessarily judging other people and merely observing, enabled me to develop a healthier relationship with my body, one that was founded on facts rather than judgment. And there is one fact that is true about everyone's body: it is an instrument through which we live. Or rather, it's an instrument through which we have the freedom to play our own music.

Standing up in front of an audience requires huge dollops of courage because it requires us to confront those aspects of ourselves that we find uncomfortable and unpleasant, such as our physical manifestation. It's far easier to cower behind the computer or the desk rather than step out in front of a sea of what we believe to be judgemental eyes. Yet it's not our audience who is judging us; rather it's us. It's our own self-critical minds that is often far crueller than even the cruellest bully in the playground. We are too often our worst enemy and before we can show up on stage we must first confront this inner bully and let it know that it's no longer acceptable to treat our bodies without anything but love and respect.

Cultivating a healthy mind

As we've already established, public speaking is an activity that can trigger all sorts of discomfort and resistance, while bringing to the surface some of our deepest and ugliest thoughts about ourselves. With such thoughts and beliefs often founded on childhood experiences, they are old and out-dated and must be weeded out. Otherwise, like an untended garden, if we don't take the time to cultivate a healthy state of mind, anxiety and other unhealthy mental habits have a way of creeping up on us, sabotaging even our best efforts.

According to beyondblue, a national initiative to raise awareness of anxiety and depression and to help people with mental disorders, 'Anxiety is the most common mental health condition in Australia. On average, one in four people – one in three women and one in five men – will experience anxiety at some stage in their life. In a twelve-month period, over two million Australians experience anxiety.' For people who suffer from anxiety or depression, public speaking is an activity that could potentially exacerbate such conditions.

It is therefore essential to invest time and energy into staying mentally healthy, whether or not you have a presentation coming up. In fact, if you are someone who has a predisposition to anxiety or other mental disorders it's vital that you have a mental health plan in place so that should an opportunity to speak in public arise, it's not something that will in anyway compromise your health. It's also important to keep in mind that there is a difference between nervousness and anxiety.

Experiencing nervousness, opposed to fear or anxiety, in the lead up to a presentation is natural and to be expected. In fact, contrary to popular belief, experiencing 'butterflies' before a presentation is actually a good thing. Nervousness before a presentation serves the purpose of reminding us that we are here to be of service to others and that our presentation is something that is important to us. Nerves, in the healthy sense, remind us that we believe in our message and we want to do the best job possible with delivering it.

Anxiety, on the other hand, is not a healthy condition, nor is it a healthy reaction to public speaking. Instead anxiety can lead to:

- Hot and cold flushes
- Racing heart
- Tightening of the chest
- Snowballing worries
- Obsessive thinking and compulsive behaviour

When faced with the prospect of having to speak in public, this can manifest as:

- Overwhelming fear about the presentation
- A desire to sabotage the event by cancelling, pretending to be sick, creating a situation so that you don't have to show up
- Procrastinating with the preparation
- Difficulty concentrating
- Profuse sweating
- Lack of sleep
- Increased restlessness, anger or irritability, especially towards anyone involved with the presentation

Unfortunately for many people, the items on this list are not uncommon experiences for people who are preparing to present. Yet cultivating a healthy mind is not something that can be done at the last minute. It requires conscious and consistent (daily) focus to ensure our thoughts are supporting all our efforts. If our thoughts are not consciously aligned with our goals and intentions, then it's all too easy for the old and out-dated conditioning to take over and sabotage even our best efforts.

It's important to cultivate a positive state of mind, especially in the face of a challenging situation such as a presentation. If a positive mental state is not your default state of mind then you will need to focus on doing whatever feels right for you in order to improve your mental state. You might start by eliminating or reducing exposure to activities such as watching the news or commercial/reality television, reading fashion magazines, or scrolling the Internet. Once you have created space within yourself from negative influences, it then becomes easier to build into your life activities that are mentally stimulating and supportive.

Engaging in physical activities has been proven to support a healthy state of mind. It doesn't matter what you do as long as it's something that gets the body moving and your heart-rate increasing. It could be walking, running, chopping wood, surfing, taking an exercise class, joining the gym, riding, yoga or swimming, but whatever it is just make sure it's something that you enjoy and derive some kind of pleasure from otherwise it's unlikely your participation will be sustained over the long term.

Another way of maintaining a healthy state of mind is to repeat positive affirmations – positive statements of intent – that support a healthy mental state and are more aligned with the kind of life you want to be living. I have a list of positive statements I repeat every morning and I always feel better after repeating them aloud a few times. Even if the statement isn't necessarily true in that moment, I know that by repeating it as if it is true increases the likelihood of its becoming true. Plus it just feels good when I'm consciously thinking healthy, positive thoughts.

Engaging presence

Recently I was listening to one of Eckhart Tolle's audio programs, *The Art of Presence.* At the beginning of the program Eckhart humorously reminded the audience that the program was *not* called 'The Art of Absence', as there's no art in being absent. This couldn't be truer when it comes to public speaking. Not only is it common for presenters to be absent on stage, it's become all too common.

Clients will share with me that while on stage they will feel like they are having an 'out of body' experience. It's as if they are on autopilot, speaking from memory rather than from a state of presence and awareness. When you're not present to what you are saying or doing, it's likely that you won't remember what you said or did. People who are not present while speaking will often have no memory of the experience once it's over. It's almost as if the presentation never happened.

Like many, I can relate to this experience. As children, we will often escape to fantasy worlds in an attempt to avoid uncomfortable situations. This is not something we do consciously but we learn fairly early on that this can be an effective coping strategy. Unfortunately, however, while this might have been an effective coping mechanism when we were younger, as adults we are actually doing ourselves and others a disservice by 'checking out'.

Being present means having our attention and focus in the present moment, regardless of whatever uncomfortable feelings might be arising. When we are present, we make ourselves available to not only our own feelings, but how others might be feeling as well. When we are present we are emotionally connected and emotional connection is what binds us to our audience and them to us.

As many of us do tend to vacate our bodies when public speaking, becoming present is an art form that, like any form of creative expression, must be practised and cultivated on a daily basis. I will often hear people say, 'I want to have more presence when I'm on stage. When I'm speaking I just don't feel like I'm getting my message across. I want more power in the way I communicate my message.' Well, if you want more presence on stage then the simple answer is you must start to cultivate presence *off* stage. You must start to develop a daily presence practice. After all, presence comes from being present, not from being perfect.

The source of power

True power originates from the present moment. It is only through our ability to be present that we are able to connect to our power, otherwise known as our potential. The word 'potential' originates from the Latin, *potentialis* or *potentia* meaning 'power' or 'potent'. Both potential and power mean 'to be able to do' and we can only do something in the present. Power and 'potency' are therefore only accessible to us when we are present in the moment. Therefore, to be powerful is to be present. The key word here is, in fact, be present.

When a presenter is present, their presentation becomes more than just an auditory experience. It becomes a total sensory experience, engaging the body, mind and spirit. The presenter is mesmerising and their words have a way of seeping beneath our conscious minds, burying themselves deep in our soul.

Dr Joe Dispenza is a wonderful example of this on-stage presence. Joe is a researcher, chiropractor, lecturer and author as well as one of the stars of the documentary movie, *What The Bleep Do We Know!?* While listening to Joe speak at an event in Sydney, I found myself so completely captivated that his presentation felt more like a meditation or a healing. Entranced, I could feel my body soaking up the words he spoke, and when his presentation finished, I felt calm and peaceful. His message was an experience he gave his audience. Now that's world-class public speaking.

Of course this is not about how we can be more like Joe or any other brilliant speaker out there. His state of presence is what makes him a powerful speaker. Your state of presence is what will make you a powerful speaker. Presence is not something you can copy, but it's something we can all cultivate.

Practising presence (not perfection)

There is literally nothing you have to do when you stand up to present. I know this sounds counterproductive to the whole premise of this book, but hear me out. The fact that you are reading this book is evidence of the life force that is currently moving through you. This life force is what is guiding your hands and fingers to hold up this book, your eyes to collect the data on the page and your brain to decode and interpret the data in order to form an understanding in your mind.

Plus, while all this is going on, your heart continues to beat, your lungs continue to inhale and exhale, and the cells in your body continue to regenerate and replenish themselves with the vital nutrients and minerals flowing through your bloodstream. To put it simply, you're already *doing* a lot. Or rather, the life force working through you is doing it.

The challenge when standing up to deliver a presentation is to trust in this life force. If this force that is within all of us is capable of keeping us alive, surely it's capable of helping us get through a presentation. If only we would surrender ourselves to it and release the controls, then it surely would.

Delivering a presentation, or even just thinking about it, is an activity that can easily take people out of the present moment. We believe that we need to do more preparation, more run-throughs, more of everything, when possibly the best thing to do at this point is to sit down and breathe. In my experience, what lets people down the most when presenting is not their lack of slides or expert information, but their lack of presence.

They are caught up in their own thoughts and not present to the moment, their message or their audience. Lack of presence robs us of our true power every time.

So rather than practising perfection we need to practise being present.

This is something I need to practise on a daily basis. Every morning as soon as I wake up I go to the couch and meditate for between thirty minutes to an hour. I haven't always woken up in this way. I used to wake up, drag myself out of bed and into the shower before getting dressed and starting my day. Once I discovered how much better I felt and how easy life became after meditating in the morning, I just kept doing it. These days, meditation is non-negotiable. If I know that I have an early start, I'll get up even earlier so I can meditate. Knowing what the benefits have been to my life from having developed a daily meditation practice, it's simply not an option *not* to do it.

A daily presence practice is something that I tell all my clients they must cultivate. It's essential. Not just for connecting to their true power as a presenter but as a person. With so much going on in our lives, we need to settle down into a space of quiet solitude and connect to the sound of our breath, the beat of our heart, the sensations in our body and the magnificence of life. When we connect to all of this, we connect to our truth. And when we present from this place, we are naturally powerful.

We all live busy lives with various restrictions on our time, therefore it's important to develop your own practice and find what suits you best. And when you find that practice, you'll wonder why you didn't do it sooner. The benefits will far outweigh any previously conceived inconvenience. A daily presence practice will be the greatest gift you ever give to yourself. But don't give yourself a hard time if you don't do it. Simply make an intention to do it the next day. Go easy on yourself.

The simplest way to help you bring your attention back to the present is by connecting to the breath. The breath is the key to the present and all the gifts and blessings contained within the present moment. The good news is we are breathing anyway. There is air coming in and out of our body all day, every day, so the hard work has already been taken care of. All we have to do is bring our focus and attention to this breath for approximately twenty minutes a day and prior to delivering a presentation.

Most of us spend our lives busy in thought while blissfully unaware of the 25,000 breaths we take and the 300,000 litres of air our lungs inhale per day. The average person (assuming we live to be eighty) will take over 700 million breaths in a lifetime, most of which will be taken unconsciously.

Thankfully, breathing is not something we need to remember to do. If we did, it's likely a few of us wouldn't be reading this right now. Our body intelligence takes care of breathing, along with all the other vital functions of the body. We are essentially free to get on with our day. Unfortunately, however, many of us waste it by worrying about things that we need not worry about, like speaking in public.

Breath supplies oxygen to the body and brain. As most people shallow breathe on a regular basis, often our body is not receiving enough oxygen to support optimal functioning. The brain requires more oxygen than any other organ in the body, and when it doesn't receive it, the result is mental fatigue, negative thoughts and lack of energy. When we become stressed or tense, this further limits the supply of oxygen, because our breathing becomes even shallower.

Presenting is a time when we need as much oxygen in our body as possible. Yet this is also the time when we become stressed and tense and end up taking short, sharp breaths. This limits oxygen supply to the brain and hinders our thinking and communication abilities, as well as our energy levels. The result is a lacklustre presentation. To deliver our best presentation, we need our brain and body to function at its optimum. Therefore, we need to learn how to breathe consciously and use our breath to bring us back to the present.

Practising conscious breathing

Practising conscious breathing isn't difficult, it doesn't have to take a lot of time and you can include the practice into your daily routine. I recommend at least five minutes of conscious breathing a day, although if you're like me and you *enjoy* the benefits of this practice, you can do it for longer. Again, you are seeking to discover what works for you.

It's important to find a quiet, comfortable place where you can sit up and close your eyes. Taking your attention to your breath, just witness the inhale and the exhale. Feel the rise and fall of your belly. Notice the sensations in your nose as the air passes through. Feel any tension in your body being released. As thoughts come in, which they will, simply let them go. Keep your attention focused on your breath until it's time to open your eyes. It's that simple!

The practice of conscious breathing is vital to becoming present as a public speaker and therefore a confident, powerful and engaging one. Your breath is your greatest ally. By relaxing our breath we relax our mind and body, and when we do this we become present to all the many opportunities the present is offering. Yet it's not a practice that you can just do once or twice and hope to receive ongoing benefits from. If you are genuinely committed to improving as a public speaker, then developing a daily breathing practice is essential. For when you know how to use your breath consciously it will serve you, not just in your presentation, but throughout your whole life.

Key 3
Plan Your Content

*The most courageous act is still to
think for yourself. Aloud.*

COCO CHANEL

S hortly after starting my own corporate training business, I received a call from a woman, Michelle, who had been given my name from a colleague and wanted to know whether I was interested in speaking at her company's management conference later in the year. She was looking for someone to run a session on developing high performance teams.

'Is this something you would be interested in?' she asked.

'Absolutely,' I said, without hesitation, even though I had no experience in developing high performing teams and wasn't particularly interested in the topic. What did excite me was the fact that she wanted *me* to speak at her management conference. As this was early on in my career, I was quite chuffed by the invitation, plus, with a new business I needed the money. Not necessarily the best reasons for agreeing to a gig.

Michelle and I chatted for a short time about the event and by the time we hung up I had secured my first official client. Feeling confident that I could deliver on the requirements Michelle had briefly outlined in our phone call, I began putting together an outline of how I envisioned the session would go.

Several weeks later, on the day of the event, I arrived at the conference centre early in order to meet Michelle, get acquainted with the environment and catch the presentation of the speaker before me. I tiptoed in, quietly taking a seat at the back of the room. Immediately I felt nausea growing in my stomach. Looking around, I estimated there were at least fifty people in the audience. I'm not sure how many I'd expected but it certainly hadn't been this many. They were also significantly older than I'd envisioned them to be. It slowly started to dawn on me that I really had no idea what to expect from the audience since I hadn't got around to asking Michelle any questions about them. I had been too excited about landing my first client to even think of anything else.

Yet the most frightening realisation was that I had totally misunderstood the brief that Michelle had outlined over the phone a month earlier. As I watched the speaker deliver a rehearsed and polished keynote to the admiring smiles and nods of his attentive audience, it was clear Michelle had requested a public speaker whereas I had organised a workshop involving group activities. Public speaking and facilitation were two very different styles of presenting and I started to have an internal meltdown.

As the speaker wrapped up his perfect presentation and applause thundered around the room, I was hit with the realisation: *I'm screwed*. And within a few minutes of introducing myself, it was clear: I was right.

A blonde woman sitting at one of the back tables with arms folded and a scowl on her face, turned and whispered something to the woman sitting next to her. Together, they began snickering quietly before capturing the attention of the rest of their table. Having lost the attention of one entire table, I ploughed on. While the rest of the room listened politely, I could feel the resistance emanating from my audience. The previous speaker had just riveted them and it was clear to every person in the room, including myself, that I had well and truly bombed. When my session finally and thankfully came to an end, the applause came more from a place of pity than anywhere else.

After the session I sat in my car, taking a moment to reflect on the experience while wondering how it had all gone so wrong. I noted that for starters, I had been so overly eager to sign my first client that I hadn't bothered to ask any further questions about the event. I hadn't taken the time to understand what my client was asking for and what the needs of the audience would be. Until the moment I walked into the conference room, I hadn't even a clue who my audience was. As a result I came barrelling in with my own set of assumptions on which my presentation was based and for which I paid the price.

Although perhaps my biggest mistake was taking on a topic that I simply wasn't truly interested in or passionate about. Perhaps, had I paid more attention to not only what my audience needed from me but also for what I felt a deep urging and passion to give, my effort might not have resulted in the train wreck that my presentation turned out to be.

Yes, it was my worst public speaking nightmare come true. And yet, it was the nightmare I needed to have. After recovering from the ordeal, I gained some incredibly useful insights that enabled me to grow and develop my abilities as a public speaker. Most importantly, I realised that the experience did not break me or my confidence. If anything, it strengthened my resolve and courage to be better.

In a practical sense, the experience also taught me the importance of taking the time to understand your audience. Without an audience you don't have a presentation. It therefore makes sense to invest some time and energy into finding out as much about them as you possibly can. As the saying goes, 'Seek first to understand, then to be understood.'

Seek first to understand

To 'understand' something means to 'stand beneath'. In other words, we must accept what you do not know and unless we have taken the time to get to know the people we are speaking in front of then we can't possibly understand and know who they are.

Getting to know your audience is a very simple exercise. It's simply a case of asking questions. Lots of them. Who will be attending? How many will there be? What do they do? Why are they there? Do they want to be there or would they prefer to be walking the dog? What do they not want? What's their experience with the topic? Do they accept and agree with, or are they resistant to the topic? Do they know each other? What do they eat for breakfast? What's their favourite colour? Okay, so perhaps you don't need to know *that* much information. But it's good to get as much appropriate information as possible.

It's also good to remember that your audiences are also people with lives outside work and business. Regardless of position or title, they are human beings with challenges and passions and hopes and dreams. They have needs and wants as well as fears and insecurities. Surprisingly, some of the most confident and successful people I have met or worked with have admitted to suffering terrible insecurities while fearing they aren't as good as everyone thinks they are.

While you can't possibly know everything about everyone in your audience, it helps to remember that they are just human beings. We all have our flaws and imperfections but most importantly, and this is good for every speaker to remember, we are all looking to fulfil the most important human need and that's the need for love and connection. If you can remember only one thing about your audience then make it this.

Freedom through structure

As a creative, I've often struggled with structure and for many years would rebel against it along with anything else that appeared to lock in and stifle my creative expression. I believed that creativity meant free rein and space in which to roam. I considered borders and boundaries to be creative blasphemy. Creativity was about being open and available to inspiration whenever it decided to drop by. There was no place in my life for structure and routine which made it difficult to hold down a regular nine-to-five job.

This structure-less approach served me well while writing for the fashion magazine in Los Angeles based on the fact that the editor left me to my own creative devices just as long as I had my stories submitted by the deadline. Unfortunately, this free-flowing approach didn't serve me as well when standing in front of the television camera in Los Angeles about to deliver my very first entertainment report. Without a script to fall back on, I had nothing to fall back on and so when I did fall I fell hard.

But sometimes we need to fall to figure out what we need in order to make sure we don't fall again. In this case, it was the importance of having some kind of plan or structure. When it comes to public speaking, especially as you're learning the craft and developing your confidence as a speaker, having structure to your ideas is not only important, it's vital.

Without structure, at least when you're starting out, you're likely to waffle and ramble and lose track of what you're attempting to communicate. Something I have come to learn and appreciate as a creative person is that structure actually creates freedom rather than limitations. Presentation structure provides a safe space in which you can move and change and adapt according to the needs of your audience. In this sense, structure becomes like a creative playground where the boundaries are more helpful than a hindrance.

A research study conducted some years ago took children onto a playing field and told them they were free to play as they wished. The one significant criteria was that there were no fences or boundaries placed around this field. The researchers found that the majority of the children remained tightly huddled near the centre of the playing field. For the second part of the study, the researchers added a boundary around the outskirts of the field. When the children were once again invited to play, the researchers found they used the field space in its entirety, playing games that took them to the edges of the field, yet still within the boundary. The study concluded that the children felt safer to explore freely once they were provided with a boundary in which to do so.

As adults, we are not that much different. In the same way children need boundaries to play freely, we need boundaries to create freely. And when it comes to public speaking, we need structure in order to speak freely. A presentation structure or 'keynote map', as I like to call it, provides boundaries in which we are free to creatively roam around and express ourselves in whatever way inspiration moves us.

The Keynote Map

The principles of structure in the public speaking sense are quite basic. Every presentation has a beginning, middle and an end. Each section within this structure contains specific elements that serve the ultimate purpose of the presentation. Now, clearly you don't need a book or a workshop on public speaking to figure this out, and yet you would be amazed at how many people fail to remember and put this into practice when presenting.

There are many different structures available to create a keynote presentation yet ultimately, they all contain the same three parts: a beginning, a middle and an ending. The elements included in each part might differ slightly so it's up to you to find what works best with your public speaking style.

The Keynote Map is an amalgamation of all the information I've picked up over the years of researching, facilitating and practising the craft of creative public speaking. This is not to say that the Keynote Map is the only way of structuring a presentation and I would suggest having a look at a variety of structures and figure out what works for you while keeping in mind the essential elements of each section.

I like to think of each section as part of an offering. The beginning, or introduction, is the wrapping paper; the middle is the gift; and the ending, or summary, is the bow that ties it all together. Each section is different, and each section is equally important. Each element of the gift supports the quality of the offering.

A question I would always ask in my workshops when discussing structure is, 'Which is the most important part of the presentation – the beginning, middle or the end?'

Usually there is a smarty-pants in the room who responds with, 'They're all important as each other.' And that would be right. Yet for the sake of the exercise, I make everyone choose only one of the three sections.

Ninety-five per cent of the people I have asked this question have said that either the beginning or the end is the most important part of a presentation. Most people would say the introduction was more important than the ending, but the debate was always between these two sections. Rarely would anyone vote for the middle section as the most important part of a presentation.

I always found this absolutely fascinating since, in my experience as a public speaking facilitator and coach, most presenters spend most of their time focused on the middle section, buried in their content. This is often at the expense of an effective introduction and conclusion. Yet when you don't frame your content with an introduction and conclusion, presentations end up being content-heavy while lacking the context for this information. Beginnings and endings are what gives something life, including a keynote presentation.

There is a popular saying for remembering the function of each section of a presentation:

1. Introduction – Tell them what you're going to tell them
2. Middle – Tell them
3. Conclusion – Tell them what you've just told them

If you can remember this, then you've pretty much grasped the fundamentals of presentation structure. Keep it simple and less is always more. Now's let's go into each section in more details.

The Introduction – The Gift Wrapping

Yusef was a participant in one of my workshops and he described the opening of a presentation like eating an apple.

'You don't put your mouth in the fruit bowl and take a bite of the apple,' said Yusef. 'You have to grab the apple first. It's the same with a presentation: you have to grab the audience's attention first.' Everyone in the room laughed when they heard Yusef's analogy because, not only was it funny, it was true. You don't jump straight into delivering your presentation. You first must grab your audience's attention, set the scene and create a context.

Openings are absolutely critical and they can make or break your presentation. It's the same with the opening scene of a movie or the first paragraph of a book. If it doesn't capture your attention within the first few minutes (in a presentation it's even sooner), chances are it's not going to hold your attention until the end. Or if you do happen to stick it out, you're not likely to remember much, if anything, once you walk out of the cinema or put the book down. It won't have captured your attention and as a result your attention will be on whatever does happen to capture it.

In the highly competitive information age in which we now live, companies and individuals are spending big dollars figuring out ways to capture your attention and then keep it. The competition for attention has increased and the standards have been raised which means we also have to raise our game when it comes to capturing our audience's attention as, if you don't get to capture it from the start, you may not have an audience at the end. While your audience might be still in the room, they will be thinking about the sandwiches waiting for them outside. You have to hook your audience in the first few seconds of your presentation and the way you do this is with a 'Creative Grab'.

The Creative Grab

'Good morning. It's a pleasure to be here. I know you're all very busy people so thank you for taking time to be here. My name is Hedley Derenzie and I'm the founder of Creative Keynote. Today I'm going to talk to you about delivering a keynote presentation with greater individual flair and creative expression....'

Zzzzzzzzz …

I'm not sure how many people would be feeling very excited about having to listen to a presentation on creative presenting if I introduced it in this way. Yet unfortunately, this is how so many people introduce themselves and their topic. Your opening needs to capture the essence of your message, and if I'm talking about being more creative when presenting in public then I would want to be a little more creative in the way I introduce this topic. I might start by saying something like:

'Good morning. Take a moment to look around at every person in the room. As you do this, you might notice all the faces in the audience. You might notice what people are wearing. Perhaps you might see someone you would like to introduce yourself to later. You might notice a lot of things but the one thing every person in this room has in common is that that there isn't a person in this room who is like anyone else. Every person in this room has something that no one else has and as a public speaker that is a valuable quality to have.

My name is Hedley Derenzie, and I'm the founder of Creative Keynote. Today I'm going to talk to you about how to be more creative in your public speaking by firstly bringing your individuality and personality to every presentation your deliver.

When did I engage my audience? The moment they started looking around the room at each other. Up to that point they had a dozen other things going on in their heads, including the email they hadn't finished, the school fees they had to pay, remembering to pick up milk on their way home, or the cute guy or girl seated in the second row. We might be offering the greatest gift in the world, but unless we have our audience's attention, they are not going to unwrap it.

The idea of the 'grab' is to create an emotional response of surprise, shock, fear, excitement, intrigue or even joy. If you can do this, you will have their attention. The challenge thereafter is to keep it. Varying theories suggest you have between seven and thirty seconds to do this. Whatever you believe to be true, the fact is you only have a moment. And in that moment, you have to connect with your audience. But keep in mind the objective is to captivate rather than coerce, to attract rather than repel, to engage rather than hound. You have to give your audience a compelling reason to come along for the ride.

Original openings require the willingness to be creative. Grab your listeners' attention by giving them an experience they won't forget. But don't forget to link your opening with your key message. Everything you do must serve the purpose you are there for.

Here are some ways to grab the attention of your audience:
- Ask a question
- Tell a brief story
- Perform an activity

- Give a demonstration
- Show a photo
- Recite a quote
- Tell a joke (make sure you claim your inner joker first!)
- State a fact or statistic

Your personal story

During the introduction of a presentation, I will always share a personal story with my audience about myself. If I'm talking about public speaking, I might share the trauma of my first TV presenting experience and about how nervous I was and how I've been able to overcome much of this fear by doing this work. I share some relevant points about my past or tell a relevant story about a recent experience that happened to me, as long as it's relevant to my audience and to the topic I'm presenting on.

The purpose of sharing personal information is to create connection, build trust and demonstrate credibility. To build trust with your audience you have to give them something of yourself. When you are on stage presenting, the visual illusion is that you are separate from your audience. Your objective in your introduction is to remind the audience that you are one of them and that you are here to be of service to them. You do this by sharing a personal story or experience that they can relate to.

Trust is not something you can ever assume you have. Nor can you assume that once you have the trust of your audience, it's yours for good. Trust is delicate and must be nurtured and respected. The greatest mistake a presenter can ever make is take their audience for granted and abusing the trust their audience gave them at the beginning of the presentation.

Your personal story is where you can demonstrate credibility. If you're an unknown speaker, the audience might be wondering why you are the one standing on stage talking to them about a particular topic. What right do you have to be there? If it's not already clear, it's up to you to demonstrate your credibility and let people know why you're the one qualified to be on stage. This doesn't mean you must have a university degree, or a hundred professional qualifications on the topic. It means you have some kind of experience, insight or understanding on the topic and it's your job to inform your audience of this. Your introduction is not the time to be shy. Yet always keep in mind, when you're talking about yourself, you are always doing it for the benefit and service of others.

Setting the Scene

Now that you've got your audience's attention and you've established trust and credibility, it's important to set the scene and outline your agenda. The reason we do this is because your audience will come into the room with expectations of their own. These expectations could be based on the presentation outline, other people's reviews, or the fact that they have no idea what they're in for. Regardless of where people's expectations originate from, your audience will have them so it's important you manage them by addressing them in the beginning.

I remember on the first evening of a weeklong yoga teacher-training course a few years back, the teacher asked everyone to write down three expectations we had for the week. At the time I thought to myself, 'I don't really have any expectations. I'm just here to get as much from the experience as possible.' But then the teacher continued.

'And don't tell me you don't have any expectations,' he told us. 'You have given up your time, your money, your families and your lives to be here for a week. You should have expectations and they should be very high.'

As I started writing my list of expectations for the week I realised that I did have expectations, even though I wasn't aware of them until being asked to write them down. Through this experience I learned that when I'm presenting, everyone in my audience will have their own list of expectations about what they are going to get from my presentation. Now, it's going to be impossible to meet everyone's different expectations especially when I don't even know what they are, which is why it's important I educate them on what my presentation is about and what they can expect at the end of it.

When we don't manage people's expectations, we risk our audience leaving disappointed. Disappointment occurs when experience doesn't meet expectations. As I mentioned in the previous section, part of getting to know my audience is to ask about their expectations. What do they want out of the session? With this information, you're in a much better position to manage your audience's expectations once you're standing in front of them.

Yet this is also the time to communicate what your expectations are of your audience. Remember, it's a two-way street. With mobile phones, laptops and every kind of iThingy at our fingertips, there are many possible distractions for a speaker to contend with. It's up to you to communicate what you need from the people in front of you. If you want people to turn their phones off, then you have to be the one to tell them. It's always better to do this upfront rather than half way through your presentation.

Here are some questions to consider when setting and managing expectations with your audience:

- What's your presentation about?
- What points are you going to cover?
- What points are you not going to cover?
- How long will you be talking?
- What should people do if they have any questions?
- Are there any resources you need to explain how to use?
- Where are the bathrooms?
- Where are the emergency exits?
- What should they do with their phones?
- What time are the breaks?
- Where will refreshments and food be available?
- Who can they talk to if they have a question?

Remember you are building a relationship with your audience and regardless of how brief this relationship might be, it's always good to get off on the right foot and to be as clear and upfront about as much as you can from as early on as possible.

The Middle – Three is Key

The middle section of your presentation is your playground. This is where you get to play with your content and ideas and the things you want to say. Now this isn't to say you can't play in the introduction and conclusion (go right ahead!) but it is in the middle section where you engage and communicate with your audience. This is where you have the freedom to let your creative juices run wild and simply have a good time. Yes, it is possible to have a good time while speaking in public.

So how many points should you have in the middle section? Well, it depends on your presentation. It will depend on the topic, the time frame and your audience's needs. If your objective, however, is to deliver your content in a way that creates a memorable impact, then the general rule is to engage the 'power of three'. Three key points will ensure your audience has a better chance of not just receiving your gift, but enjoying the value, having retained the information.

Three has been the magic number ever since we were little kids. We have the three little pigs, three blind mice, three Billy Goats Gruff, Goldilocks and the three bears, and let's not forget, *The Three Stooges*. In numerology, the number three represents creativity and communication. When we utilise the power of three, we connect to our capacity to be bright, effervescent and sparkling, with an ability to share our talents and creatively express ourselves. Three is a powerful number, yet perhaps its greatest benefit is that it's easy for the human brain to remember chunks of information that have been broken down into three.

The general rule in presentation structure is to keep your points to three. Now, if you can't distil your content into three key points, then a good option is to work with multiples of three because it's far easier for our brains to recall information when presented in blocks of three. Therefore if you need more than three points, then aim for either six points or nine points. I wouldn't recommend having any more than nine points in your presentation, as people simply won't remember them. Instead, it's likely they will remember the last three points only.

Remember we live in a world of information overload and our capacity to retain facts over the long term has been reduced. It's a good idea to master the art of distilling your content which means being cruel with your content in order to be kind to your audience. In general always stick to the rule of three and make your message easy and accessible to your audience. When it comes to public speaking, less really is always more.

Let's say, for example, I'm delivering a keynote presentation on 'Creative Public Speaking'. My three key points would be:

1. What is Creative Keynote Speaking?
2. The Creative Keynote Process
3. Becoming a Creative Keynote Speaker

How easy is it do you think for people to remember these points? Pretty easy. By keeping it simple for your audience to remember your points of your presentations means they are likely to remember the information associated with each point. Our brain is like a filing system and it helps to deliver information in a way that supports this mental filing system, making it easy to retain and recall information when required.

If you have an overabundance of content, sometimes it can be difficult to not only identify your key points but to drill them down to three. If this is the case, I suggest getting everything in your head down on paper and then apply the 'Need versus Nice' rule. This means for every point on your piece of paper, ask yourself, 'Is this a point the audience *needs* to know or is it a point that would be *nice* for them to know?'

Once you've done this, toss out all the 'nice' points. Only give your audience what they absolutely need to know and try and do it within three key points. Sure it might be nice to shower your audience with all your wonderful insights and knowledge, but you're only doing yourself and your audience a disservice. Give your audience what they need and in return they will be an attentive and appreciative audience.

Conclusions – Tying the Bow

When delivering a gift, it's a good idea to wrap the gift completely since a half-wrapped gift is often a half-baked one. The same is true for a presentation. When you are delivering a presentation, it's important to deliver it complete. This means having a conclusion as well as an introduction. A conclusion is like the ribbon around the gift. It finishes the presentation off nicely and completes the experience.

A conclusion is as important as both the introduction and the middle yet unfortunately, this is where many public speakers fall short. When it comes to a presentation, being proficient in two out of the three sections doesn't really cut it. To deliver an impactful and inspirational presentation means you must have all three sections working. If you're missing even one of these then your presentation will be incomplete.

Have you ever heard of a presenter finishing with something like this: 'Okay folks, well, it looks like I'm out of time. Any questions?'

Unfortunately this is a common end to many presentations even though it's not technically an ending. It's just an abrupt cutting off of the presentation at the middle. Your closing needs to be as powerful as your opening and your middle sections. Keep in mind, your conclusion is your last point of contact with your audience and what they are likely to remember most. You want to leave your audience wanting more which means crafting a conclusion that is going to facilitate some kind of ongoing relationship.

To give an effective conclusion, you must include a quick summary of your key points, an invitation to act, some time for questions and an emotional anchor that brings it all together. Ideally you want people feeling differently than how they felt at the beginning of your presentation. Remember, you've just taken people on a journey and you're now at the end of that journey. It's important to finish it properly.

A quick summary

As you did in the introduction, remind your audience of everything you've just talked about. In other words, tell them what you've just told them. By doing this you are reminding them of your key points and reinforcing these ideas in their hearts as well as their minds. A quick summary is like packaging your ideas into a neat little box and handing it to your audience, making it easier for them to access again once they have left the room.

An invitation to act

Having put so much effort into preparing and delivering your presentation, what is it you now want your audience to do with the information you have shared with them?

Recently, I saw a presenter give an incredibly inspiring speech to over 400 people. Afterwards, when asking a few people in the audience what they thought, the general response was, 'I loved it but I don't really know what to do next.' Don't miss the opportunity to make a difference. Your audience is waiting for your instruction. They want you to tell them what to do with the information and how they can make practical use of it. By inviting them to action, you are engaging with them in a relationship outside of your presentation and you are showing them how to derive value from your gift.

An emotional anchor

A powerful way of doing this is to link it back to something you shared in your introduction. It could be a story, a photograph, an inspirational quote or the coming together of a metaphor that you've weaved in throughout your presentation. An emotional anchor is a feeling the audience can hold onto once they leave the room. This emotion holds the memory of your presentation, including the information associated with it. It's enables them to draw on your presentation long after it is over. An emotional anchor creates a sense of completion, rounding off your presentation in a powerful and memorable way.

Questions and answer time

If part of your presentation requires you to take questions from the audience, you can choose to see this in one of two ways: as something to be feared because of the element of the unknown, or as a wonderful way to deepen your connection with your audience and solicit feedback as to whether your gift has been received and understood.

Questions are an unknown factor in a presentation and can make presenters nervous. While you can prepare to answer questions you might be asked, you can never know exactly what is going to happen until it's actually happening. Therefore, presence and knowing how to remain calm and focused becomes critical. And of course if you find yourself in a situation where you don't know the answer to a question, don't be afraid to say so. It can be more appealing to appear human and willing to learn along with the audience than to appear closed off and isolated in your expertise.

Managing your time

Time is a completely different experience when speaking in public. One thing that I have found is that time goes a lot faster on stage than it does in everyday life. Thirty minutes of speaking may sound like a lifetime when you're preparing for your presentation, yet is likely to feel like thirty seconds once on stage, therefore it's important to manage your time accordingly.

When it comes to time management, a good rule is to apply the 80/20 rule, or in Creative Keynote terms, the 10/80/10 rule. That is, you will spend 10 per cent of your time in the introduction, 80 per cent in the middle and the remaining 10 per cent in the conclusion. These are approximate guides. For example, a thirty-minute presentation will entail a three to five-minute introduction, a twenty-minute middle and a three to five-minute conclusion.

If you find yourself halfway through your presentation and you're running out of time, don't rush your way through your content. Cut your content from the middle section. Never cut time from your introduction or conclusion. Remember, your introduction and conclusion give your presentation context. Without context, your middle section won't make sense, so rather than compromise content, be willing to skip over some of your points and finish strongly instead.

There's nothing worse than a presenter who is speaking a million miles an hour while flicking through a bunch of slides in a race to finish within the given time frame. Public speaking is not a race. Remember, you're offering your audience a gift which has to be delivered in a specific time frame. By planning your presentation and using the structure provided, you are in a better position to manage your time appropriately. Managing your time is a delicate art but it can be done

Key 4

Personalise Your Points

*I want to make people cry even when
they don't understand my words.*

EDITH PIAF

At a Sydney Festival several years ago, I had the privilege of listening to an author called JB Rowley share a remarkable personal story. On 7th February 2009, Rowley had been at home in Victoria when a series of out-of-control bushfires ripped through the state, killing 173 people and injuring 414 on what the rest of the country would come to know as 'Black Saturday'. While Rowley had remained safe in her home that afternoon, the impact of the fires inspired her to do something to help the devastated communities. Rowley, along with several others, organised a series of free dinners for people in the affected regions in an effort to support those whose lives had been changed forever.

In the small town of Flowerdale, 200 homes had been lost and thirteen residents had died in the fires. During one of the dinners in Flowerdale several months after the fires, JB heard about the 'Flowerdale tattoo' and was intrigued. The following day she ventured over to the community hall to find out more. There she met a woman called Odette, who held out her forearm revealing a tattoo of a blackened tree stump with a single green leaf growing out of the trunk. Odette explained to JB that she got the tattoo because she wanted a permanent reminder of the events of 'Black Saturday'.

Odette shared with JB that, as news of her tattoo spread throughout the small neighbourhood, some of the other Flowerdale residents decided they also wanted a permanent reminder of all they had survived. As JB described, 'Pretty soon there were busloads of Flowerdale residents heading down to Melbourne to the tattooist, who was generously donating her services to anyone from Flowerdale who wanted to have the tattoo.' JB told us there were now at least eighty-five Flowerdale residents who shared the black tree tattoo, including whole families and an eighty-year-old grandmother! The tattoo was a dual symbol of remembrance of the past and hope for the future. The image, as well as the experience, has united the Flowerdale community, which is now stronger than ever before.

JB finished by saying, 'Although the black tree is not tattooed on my body, its story is etched in my memory. It has been a symbol of community and proof of the power of hope since 2009, and it will continue to be in 2011 and beyond.'

Thanks to JB's story, the image of the Flowerdale tattoo is now etched in my own memory. I have since listened to JB's story online a number of times, written about it for my column in *Nature & Health* magazine, and am sharing it with you now. This is the power of stories. When they move us, they stay with us. We pass them on. They move others. Stories that live in our hearts stay alive in the hearts of others.

JB could have told us her story by reading from a script. Instead she invited us to join her in the experience as she spoke openly and honestly. She stood at the front of the stage and spoke to us, like a friend. She invited us to the dinner celebrations with people who had lost everything; she introduced us to Odette and revealed the powerful image of the Flowerdale tattoo. JB took us on a tour of the town, where houses were being rebuilt and trees were being reborn, and she also showed us the hope now living in the hearts of the Flowerdale residents. JB's story moved us, not just because the story was moving, but because the story had moved *her*. She invited us to be a part of that experience by encouraging us to feel it too.

One of the reasons this story had such a powerful impact on me is because my father passed away from cancer six days later. On the Saturday the fires raged through Victoria, I recall walking past the television screen in the living room as I carried trays of food upstairs to my father and looking in horror at the images that were captioned with a newsfeed of the increasing death toll. I remember contemplating how precious life was and how quickly it can be taken away from us.

We don't know how our stories will impact our audience. All we know is that they will. Stories are powerful bridges between the rational and the emotional. They are the heartbeat of our presentations, because they bring our information to life. They make concepts and key points real and relatable because stories, especially those taken from our own life experience, are emotional. Without stories, our presentations appeal to our intellect, yet for our gift to be of any real value we need it to capture the hearts of our audience as well as their minds. After all, no one does anything until they *feel* something and it's our job as presenters to create that emotional experience for our audience. To do this we must become, not just public speakers, but *storytellers*.

The purpose of storytelling

Most of us know how to tell a good story, having collected a mental library full of the kind that we know will generate the applause and validation we're all longing for. Over time, we've rehearsed and refined our best stories until we can rattle them off like a shopping list. For many of us, storytelling is something that we've always been able to do and over the years is something we think we've become pretty good at. After all, we've been telling stories ever since we can remember.

Yet these days storytelling, especially in presentations, seems to have become a required skill and as a result our stories have become so manufactured and manicured that we have forgotten what they actually *feel* like. We use tools like humour to hide the uncomfortable parts and skip over the bits that are simply too painful to share; we gloss over the not-so-pretty details and trim the unkempt corners of anything we might find shameful or embarrassing. Or we just make the whole thing up in order to prove a point.

In other words, we have become disassociated from our own stories. Sure they might get a laugh but often will fail to do much more than that.

I know all about this kind of storytelling. Several years into my career as a facilitator, I started to long for a deeper, more connected experience to public speaking. For years I'd been helping people overcome their fear of public speaking yet the truth was, I was still terrified of it. Yes, I had come a long way from that pivotal moment in front of the television camera in Los Angeles, but I had not yet confronted my own fears and insecurities that lay buried just beneath the surface. It had become easier to help other people deal with their fears than it was to deal with my own. I wanted to go beyond the basics – how to gesture appropriately and make effective eye contact – and to take the participants on a journey of self-discovery. Yet to do this meant I first had to be willing to go there myself. Consequently, I enrolled in a five-day public speaking retreat in New Mexico in the United States, flying to the other side of the world in the hope of finally facing and overcoming my fears.

On the first morning of the retreat, our facilitator Gail informed our intimate group of six that we were to think of a personal story which we would then stand up and share with the group. I knew exactly the story I was going to share. It was the story of how I acquired the scars on my stomach, arms and throat. It's a story I knew well because I had told it so many times, having perfected my delivery to get the laughs followed by the applause at the end. It was a story that would inevitably make me look good, which in this case, meant looking like a confident public speaker.

When my turn came around, I stood up at the front of the room and began telling my story. I was fourteen years old and participating in a work experience program at a health retreat on the Gold Coast in Queensland. During my five weeks there, I befriended the only other girl on the program, and my roommate, Didee, who was several years older. Each week we were given a day off, during which we would either hitch a lift into town or go to the beach. One Sunday I suggested we do something different.

'How about we go horse riding?' I said. I had noticed a mob of brumby horses in a nearby paddock that had recently been fenced with barbed wire.

'But we haven't got any riding equipment,' said Didee.

'Don't worry,' I said. 'I've got an idea.'

We trekked up the hill to the paddock where several of the wild horses were grazing quietly. Without reins, a saddle or even a rope, I explained to Didee that we would sneak up to one of the more mellow-looking horses and I would grab onto its mane, throw my leg over and haul myself up before grabbing onto Didee and pulling her up behind me. It wasn't the best thought out plan but I figured we would make it work. Somehow. And surprisingly we did.

Didee and I threw ourselves onto the back of a brown and white horse which then set off at a gallop towards a tree with several low-hanging branches. As we hurtled towards the tree, it became apparent that our horse had a plan of its own. It was heading straight towards the tree in the hope the branches would knock us off its back. We had possibly chosen one of the more intelligent horses in the pack, as this is exactly what happened. The branch collected both of us and sent us hurtling through the air, returning to the ground, which is clearly where the horse thought we belonged. After realising that neither of us was hurt, we burst into fits of laughter before creeping up to the horse once more to have another go.

This time our horse was no longer grazing quietly. Instead, it was standing to attention, its ears pricked back and its left hoof tilted forward as if ready for anyone who wanted to try that stunt again. Ignoring the clear signs to stay back from the animal, we slowly moved forward before I once again leaned in and grabbed the horse's mane, only to find the horse was off bolting down the paddock with me clinging to the side while Didee watched from an increasing distance. Bypassing the tree, the horse was now barrelling at full speed towards the newly erected barbed wire fence. I knew this was not going to end well.

As the horse rounded the wooden fence post and began galloping along the side of the fence, the barbed wire was now inches from my body. Once again the horse knew exactly what it was doing. As the last strands of mane slipped through my desperate fingers, I felt myself captured in space for a brief moment before slamming against the wooden pole and ricocheting into the mass of barbed wire. That's when everything went black.

As my eyes fluttered open, I could hear someone calling my name. I saw Didee standing over me with a stricken expression on her face.

'Don't move,' she said, which wasn't going to be a problem. I could taste blood. My eyes fell shut and I sank back into blackness as the sounds of Didee running down the paddock to get help faded into the distance. Several hours and a painful hospital visit later, I was back at the health retreat, covered in bandages and with stitches in my arm and throat. The managing director suggested I stay in my room so as not to upset any of the guests. Apparently my injuries were not good for business.

Two decades later at the retreat in New Mexico, I pulled up the sleeve of my shirt to reveal the scars that were still evident. The group leaned in as I shared how these scars were a reminder to never lose the courage to take risks but to perhaps take more calculated and measured risks. Yet my scars were also a tribute to the brash fourteen year old who wasn't afraid to throw herself on the back of a wild horse. Surely there's some strength in that.

As I finished sharing my story, the group gave me an enthusiastic round of applause and I returned to my chair feeling pleased with my efforts. The audience laughed in all the right places and appeared to be impressed. I waited eagerly for Gail to share with me her feedback, which would no doubt be positive.

'That's a great story, Hedley,' she said as I settled back into my seat in preparation to be praised. 'You tell it really well.'

'Thank you,' I said, beaming.

'But you know what?' Suddenly I wasn't feeling so sure of myself. 'While it's a great story and you tell it really well, I can also tell you've told that story many times before. It's a *safe* story. I say 'safe' because you know how to tell it in a way that is going to get the reaction you want from your audience.'

I nodded in agreement since everything she was saying was true.

'Over the next four days, I want you to experiment by telling the stories you've never told before,' Gail continued. 'Let's see what happens when you reveal those other parts of yourself that you haven't yet exposed to the world.'

Gail's words resonated deeply with me. In her kind and gentle way, she was the first person to invite me into that deeper, more connected experience of public speaking I'd been yearning for. She did this by encouraging me to share parts of myself that I'd never shared in front of an audience. In other words, she was asking me to be vulnerable, something I wasn't yet familiar with. Certainly not on stage in front of other people. This, I realised, lay at the core of my fear of public speaking.

The fact was I was terrified of revealing who I really was behind my well-rehearsed stories that had been told a million times before and which only served to feed my need for validation and approval from my audience. I was afraid that if I was just myself on stage people would reject and judge me and so, over the years, I had created a persona that protected me from this. Yet all this does is serve to intensify the fear that at some stage someone is going to see straight through it and know it's all an act, which of course it is.

One of the most powerful things I learned from that five-day retreat is that true power in presenting comes from our willingness to reveal ourselves in our presentations. I'm not talking about revealing our deepest, darkest secrets, but we must at least be willing to share some of our personal experiences. Sure, it's fine to deliver an interesting presentation filled with interesting facts and interesting research and interesting statistics, but such a presentation will only ever be … interesting. A truly inspiring and memorable presentation, one that moves people to change their behaviours and take action for a cause, is one with emotion. And the one thing that will inject emotion into all those interesting facts is our stories. And the more personal our stories are, the more powerful our presentations become.

This is the purpose of storytelling. Stories create emotional connection and storytelling is all about building this emotional connection with our audience. Yet to become a true storyteller in this sense we have to first connect to that place within ourselves where our stories live. In other words, we have to be willing to connect to our emotional side and then bring this part of ourselves into our speaking. After all, stories are just energy in motion. It's our stories that give energy to our information and bring our presentations to life.

Becoming a storyteller

When I begin a new workshop, I often ask each member of the group to share an interesting personal fact. There are always a few surprise responses such as, 'I'm a world champion ballroom dancer' or, 'In my spare time I like to study ants' or some other unique responses which are usually followed by a barrage of further questions or some good-hearted laughter. And yet these responses are not the norm.

In my experience, most people will respond with a comment along the lines of, 'Um, I don't know. I'm not really that interesting.'

Let me be clear on one thing: if you're alive, you're interesting!

You might not think you're interesting because you live with yourself all day, every day, and you have since the moment you were born. But the rest of the world hasn't and the rest of the world hasn't had your experiences. We don't know what you know, we haven't shared your insights and we don't know what it's like to look through your eyes. These are your stories and yes, they *are* interesting because no one knows what it's been like to walk through life in your shoes. Only you do.

What might be boring and commonplace to one person is often incredibly interesting and fascinating to another. To become better storytellers we have to accept this for ourselves. We must own our stories as part of our unique and original expression – and by owning them, I mean seeing our stories as valuable and worthy. It's important to recognise that the situations and events we experience and which we become conscious of happening around us are significant. They are literally creating our lives in every moment.

It might help to remember that no one on the planet has had the combination of experiences you've had. No one has lived the life you have lived, not even your siblings. Your life is a series of stories and as long as we are breathing, we are continuing to develop and add to the series.

When we see our stories as a gift, we no longer limit ourselves to only the fabulous tales that serve to make us look good. We are full of meaningful experiences where we have discovered pain, heartbreak, joy, success, failure, the overcoming of adversity, awakenings and powerful insights. The further we are willing to explore our personal stories, the more stories we have to choose from when it comes to making a point or delivering some information in a new and creative way.

The willingness to be vulnerable

What makes you vulnerable makes you beautiful.
- Brené Brown, Ph.D, LMSW

Our stories are only as powerful as our willingness to be honest with our storytelling. Vulnerability is the courage and willingness to reveal our emotional truth. According to author Brené Brown in her book, *Daring Greatly: How the Courage to Be Vulnerable Transforms the Way We Live, Love, Parent and Lead*, 'Vulnerability is the core, the heart, the center, of meaningful human experiences.' As Brené goes on to define it, vulnerability is 'uncertainty, risk and emotional exposure.' Sounds like a walk in the park, right? Okay, perhaps not. Yet the willingness to be vulnerable with your audience will not only connect you more with them, it will serve to transform this fear of public speaking so many of us experience. As we already know, the fear of public speaking is not necessarily fear but rather a sense of shame that if we reveal who we truly are, the world will reject us.

It's fair to say that to be vulnerable, especially in a public setting, does requires courage – a good healthy dose of it. To reveal ourselves honestly and truthfully in the presence of another, for many of us, is one of our biggest challenges. Yet with challenges come their rewards and, speaking from personal experience, the times when I have surmounted that challenge and revealed my personal side with my audience are the times that have been the most rewarding. It draws people closer rather than pushing them away. Vulnerability creates bridges between hearts where before there was nothing.

As we grow up we learn, unfortunately, that to be vulnerable means to risk being ridiculed, rebuked, rejected or cast out of the pack. When we are young, this is the absolute worst thing that can happen. As kids, we learn (sometimes fast) to buckle up and knuckle down, doing whatever we think we need to do to fit in. While this may have served us in the school playground, it doesn't serve us on the stage in front of a room full of people.

When I was about six years old I remember seeing former Prime Minister Bob Hawke choke up on television during a speech. I couldn't believe what my little eyes were seeing. The Prime Minister of Australia was crying. Suddenly this man and I had something in common. While I didn't understand anything about politics or what he was saying, the fact that he was crying meant that he was like me and from that moment on I became fond of Mr Hawke. Later when I learned that Mr Hawke had been talking about his daughter's drug addiction, and his own infidelity, I felt even greater admiration for him. It takes a person of considerable courage and strength to be so open and vulnerable in such a public setting.

Unfortunately we don't often see such signs of vulnerability in public situations and these days, our political and corporate leaders have been trained within an inch of their lives by media and presentation 'experts' on how to 'stay on topic' or deflect the point altogether. As a result, this is how most of us learn to speak and present in public. We learn from watching those already doing it even though it's an entirely manufactured performance.

Recently I saw an interview on television with a prominent female executive who was clearly well versed in handling the media and presenting her agenda. After a few minutes, it didn't feel like it was an interview at all; rather it was a well-rehearsed act. While there were two people sitting opposite each other engaging in what looked to be an interview, there was no sharing, there was no authentic discourse and there was certainly no genuine expression of vulnerability. It was a very boring three minutes of television and it was anything but inspiring.

Having worked with corporate clients who have to speak in public on a regular basis, no matter how factually interesting their presentations are, corporate presenters are at risk of hiding behind facts and figures and corporate speak because this is the way it's always been done. Unfortunately there is still a very strong cultural conditioning that it's not professional to bring your own personality and personal stories into a corporate presentation. Thankfully this is changing and corporate presentations are becoming more engaging because presenters recognise the need to take risks and connect with their audiences on a more authentic level.

As creative professionals working in creative industries, there is certainly more freedom to express oneself in a more emotional way. Yet it can still be a daunting task. It's important to remember that every opportunity to speak to a group of people is an opportunity to inspire change, and this can only be done with the willingness and the courage to invest our heart and soul into what is ultimately a personal offering.

Accepting the risks

Yes, there are risks with being vulnerable. By revealing something personal about yourself, there's a chance you could find yourself being rejected or ridiculed or shunned by those you are being vulnerable with. But what's the alternative? You either keep yourself safe by keeping your emotional side out of it and sticking to the facts for the sake of keeping other people – the kind of people who might reject and ridicule you – happy? Now, that doesn't sound like much of a pay-off.

A client once asked, 'What if I show my vulnerability and people use it against me?' It had happened to her before and she wasn't about to put herself in such a position again. Unfortunately my client was working in a toxic work environment that was never going to change until someone found the courage to take a risk and speak openly and honestly about what was happening. There's no question, this takes courage but the rewards often far outweigh such risks.

Often the risks of being vulnerable are simply in our own minds and our resistance to this is a case of our ego attempting to protect us. It takes tremendous courage to be vulnerable, especially in a public setting such as a presentation, but in my experience and the experience of those I've worked with, the benefits of being vulnerable have far outweighed any perceived risks.

The other misconception we have about revealing our vulnerabilities is that if we allow ourselves to be honest and reveal our emotional side, we might 'lose the plot'. That is, we fear that we might start to cry or choke up in the middle of a presentation and not be able to recover. I remember when Gail challenged me to share some of my more vulnerable stories during the public speaking retreat, my mind began to go crazy with questions. *What if I can't control myself? What if I start crying and can't talk? What if I forget what I'm talking about? What if I make a fool of myself? What if I look stupid in front of everyone? What if I end up in a heaving, humiliated pile of snot on the floor? What if? What if? What if?*

Ultimately, what we fear is losing control. Yet accepting that we are not in control is the essence of vulnerability. We don't necessarily have the answer; we might have made a mistake or got it wrong or have no idea how to move forward. Vulnerability is the ability to say, 'I don't know' or, 'I messed up'. That's why it's so powerful. We are letting down our guard and showing our tenderer, more emotional side – the part of ourselves that isn't in control and doesn't always have everything together.

One of the most beautiful memories I have of that retreat is a woman sharing an intimate story with the audience. As she told her deeply personal story, her eyes began to moisten and tears began to slide down her cheeks. *Oh my God, she's crying!* I thought. She was living out my public speaking nightmare. I couldn't think of anything worse than speaking in front of an audience and suddenly starting to cry. It was one of the biggest reasons I resisted sharing personal stories on stage. Yet

I watched in complete awe and wonderment as this woman continued sharing her story while experiencing her emotions so elegantly. She didn't lose it or break down. She simply continued talking through the tears, which soon turned to laughter as her story took a new turn.

As the woman's emotions moved freely through her, they moved through us, the audience. We felt everything she was feeling. One minute we all had tears streaming down our cheeks and the next we were laughing with her. As she spoke through her sadness and she spoke through her joy, we listened and experienced all of it with her. It was a beautiful and breathtaking example of how the power of vulnerability can transform a simple story into an emotional and memorable experience.

Vulnerability as a public speaker does require willingness but it also helps to have a little bit of faith that when you show up and reveal you're not perfect (heavens no!) that you won't suddenly be struck by lightning and fall in a heap only to have the rest of the world kick you in the guts. The fact is the chances of this happening are very, very slim.

But the only way you're going to know for yourself is if you accept the risks, and give it a go. You won't know just how safe you are with your audience until you're willing to give up the need to look good in the eyes of others and get a little personal. The rewards for taking this risk is that you're likely to feel so much better about yourself, less afraid of speaking in public and more connected to your audience. These are just some of the many rewards you will find yourself experiencing when you choose to be vulnerable.

Sharing our personal stories

By being vulnerable I'm not talking about turning your next presentation into a 12-Step meeting where you divulge your most intimate details about yourself. Being vulnerable and opening yourself to sharing more of your personal experiences with your audience is for three reasons: connection, connection and connection. Okay, so that's one reason but it is an important reason.

Sharing a personal story or experience in your presentation must still be for the higher purpose of your presentation. It must serve to complement your key message and create context for the key point you are highlighting. Storytelling is not about indulging yourself in the sound of your own voice or showing off in any way. A story must always serve the message you are attempting to communicate. You must always be serving the audience in everything you say and do.

A wonderful example of this is set by Andrew Griffiths. Andrew is a bestselling author, public speaker and all-round great guy. One of the many books he has written is The Me Myth, in which he shares the story of his difficult upbringing along with some of the harder choices he was required to make to live the life he's living today. With the challenges that Andrew faced early on it would have been so easy for him to fall into addiction and violence, yet he chose a life of inspiration, purpose and love.

Andrew shares his personal story in his books and presentations not to seek sympathy or play the victim, but to create an instant connection with his audience. He knows that by revealing these parts of himself, others will feel more connected to him. Andrew realises that he can have a lot more impact and influence in the world when connected to others.

As an author and a speaker, I've also had the experience of sharing personal aspects of myself. While at times it's been difficult and hasn't always gone smoothly, I've come to recognise that the more I reveal about myself and my life, the more connected I feel to others and the more connected they feel to me. Personal stories create a common link with people because we can all relate to difficulties and challenges we have had to face. Someone might not have experienced exactly the same challenges and difficulties as I have, but the essences remain the same.

Sharing personal stories and experiences is important. It's equally important to assess our stories and ensure they are relevant to our message and the purpose we are aiming to fulfil.

Personal versus Private

In today's world we have become accustomed, perhaps even immune, to people spilling their guts out all over the television and Internet, revealing every nook and cranny of their personal lives. Reality shows such as *Keeping Up With The Kardashians, The Real Housewives of Orange Country* (and all the other locations), *Jersey Shore* and many more have helped to create this culture that says it's okay to air your dirty laundry in public. In fact, it can lead to fortune and fame.

Public speaking is not about acquiring fortune and fame and just because everyone is doing it, doesn't make it right. Fame and fortune and other benefits may be a by-product of your speaking career, but it's not the reason behind it. The sharing of your personal story is for the purpose of creating a heart-based connection with your audience. It's not about vomiting up every private thought you've ever had for the purpose of creating shock value. Public speaking is not an attention-seeking sport.

When you're developing as a public speaker it's important to know when and where to draw the line between personal information (stories that are acceptable for the public domain) and private information (which is information to be kept between yourself and your inner circle). Always remember that the purpose of sharing your personal story, or at least parts of it, is to create an opening with your audience where a connection needs to be made. You want to invite your audience into your life, but as a guest – not a permanent resident.

Engaging visual aids

> *Create your own visual style. Let it be unique*
> *for yourself and yet identifiable for others.*
> **- Orson Welles**

On the dot of nine, Gary our trainer, pulled up a swivel chair, swung it around so his back was facing us and he was facing the computer screen and (to my horror) began reciting the words on his PowerPoint slides. At first I thought Gary was kidding, demonstrating how not to run an adult education workshop. After all, this was the first day of the *Workplace Training and Assessment* qualification program. Yet as Gary kept on reading his slides line by painful line, occasionally swivelling his chair around to check we were still paying attention (we weren't), I realised he wasn't joking. Instead, Gary was unintentionally demonstrating how to abuse the craft of public speaking through the over-reliance on their PowerPoint slides.

Meanwhile, Kim, a participant in one of my workshops, expressed her own reliance on visual aids to compensate for her fear and the impact it had on her audience's receptivity of her presentation, explaining that the only way she could get through her presentation was by overusing slides.

'I made a very wordy PowerPoint presentation, stood in a crowded room and just read word for word from the slides,' she told us. 'It was a train wreck. I watched as eyes glazed over and boredom dulled everyone's faces. I didn't have the guts to change things in the middle of the presentation so I just kept going, right up to the end. The applause was as if to say, "Thank goodness she's finished!".' To Kim's credit, she could see the error of her ways and wasn't afraid to admit it. We all laughed as she recounted her experience because it was something to which we could all relate.

The dark sides of slides

PowerPoint, with all its wizardry genius and animation and ability to bring monotonous facts and figures to life, has a dark side that has only emerged with its overuse. As the human element of presentations was reduced to a dark figure positioned off to one side, presentations became dull, boring and monotonous. They lacked the emotional colour and animation that connected the information to the heart of audience. In fact, PowerPoint had gone from revolutionising presentations to ripping the heart right out of them.

It's no wonder that people walk into a conference room framed by a giant white square in the centre of the wall and groan with despair, knowing it's going to be a long, uncomfortable day. And with so many screens now located in the centre of the room, it's actually *expected* that the PowerPoint slides are the focus of the presentation. Meanwhile the presenter can hang off to the side with a clicker, a coffee and a cupcake without anyone noticing. While this might be a relief for the presenter, it's certainly no relief for the audience. It's as if we have been conditioned to feel bored before the presentation has even begun. And while PowerPoint and Apple's equivalent, Keynote, do have benefits for presentations in supporting the delivery of information, their brilliance has been lost in our inability to use these programs properly.

When we look at the history of PowerPoint slides and how they were created, it's not surprising we've lost our way as public speakers. Back in 1987, Apple created a program called Presenter, the aim being to provide people with the ability to use computer-generated slides to support their presentations (the key word here being 'support'). Bill Gates, knowing a good thing when he saw it, swooped in and bought the idea from Apple. Presenter became Microsoft PowerPoint and the software quickly became a worldwide phenomenon for the reason that the folks at Microsoft knew exactly what they were doing when marketing this new software, playing directly into people's fear of public speaking. Microsoft PowerPoint attempted to revolutionise the way people delivered their presentations by making the presenter – the human and emotional link between the content and the audience – redundant. For those harbouring a deep-seated fear of public speaking, PowerPoint was a gift from the heavens. And presenters certainly didn't waste time in making good use of this 'gift'. No longer did people need to feel like they were being burnt at the stake every time they stood at the front of the room; with PowerPoint they realised they could torture their audience instead! Afraid of making eye contact with your audience? No problem. Just read through those 134 fascinating slides and you won't have to.

Changing the way we use slides

For the nervous presenter, I understand the attraction of PowerPoint or Apple's Keynote. For those who would rather rest their hands on a hot stove than bear the torture of standing up in front of an audience to speak, overusing slides is a very attractive option. I too am guilty of overusing slides to compensate for my fear. After all, slides are a wonderful way to take the audience's attention off yourself by placing them into a long, deep sleep from which they will wake having not remembered a single word of what you've said. If you want to bore your audience to death then by all means, whack a few hundred PowerPoint slides together and click through them at a very fast rate, and you'll have them unconscious in no time. Although if you're wanting to use the craft of public speaking to deliver a powerful message that could make a meaningful difference to people's lives, then we are going to have to start using our slides a little differently.

The good news is that as creative people, this shouldn't be too difficult. Plus having understood that presenting is an offering and that every opportunity to speak in public is the opportunity to share the gifts we have, we can now start incorporating and using slides in the way they were originally designed for: to support the message. Visual aids are just that: visual aids. Remember that when you are using slides sparingly, you are sparing your audience and instead, maintaining a meaningful and personal connection with them.

When using slides appropriately and effectively, photographs and visual images are often more powerful than words. If you choose to use slides in your presentation I strongly recommend you use relevant and interesting photographs and visual images, as they are a great way to engage the senses and enhance the emotional response we are already generating through our personal interaction with the audience. As the adage goes, 'A picture is worth a thousand words.'

A friend of mine told me about a presentation he had given to the all-male board of his company on the importance of alignment (as several of the new board members were out of alignment with the company's long-term vision). He started his talk by showing a photograph of a man standing at a urinal. He then turned to his audience and said, 'Well gentlemen, I think you would all agree that alignment is something that is absolutely critical in life and that's what I'm here to talk to you about today.' It was a fantastic way to open what was going to be a challenging presentation. Everyone laughed, which brought the group into immediate alignment and not surprisingly, my friend went on to deliver a great presentation that resulted in a successful outcome. It should probably be noted that this introduction might not have the same impact if there were any women in the room!

If you do have to use words on your slides then keep them to a minimum. You might think, 'But I use my slides as a reminder of what to say next.' As you've probably figured out by now, this is not what it means to honour your audience and deliver a creative keynote presentation. Your audience can read your slides at home. They have come to see and hear you. When preparing your content, you must constantly be asking yourself, 'How can I present this information in a more creative way for the benefit of my audience?'

While there are 'no rules' to delivering your content, here are some points to keep in mind:

- Keep your slides to an absolute minimum
- Ideally, only use photographs, images or graphics
- If you do have to use text, only use key words

Remember, lots of information on a slide is neither interesting nor original, and it's certainly not creative. You know your topic, you know your key message and you know your key points. You know how to bring your stories to life when you tell them. Your presentation slides are there to complement you and what you have to say, but they are not there to replace you. Always remember this when putting your slides together. Visual aids are simply meant to aid the delivery of your presentation rather the deliver your presentation for you.

Be Creative

Of course, slides are not the only visual aids available as support mechanisms for our message. There is a variety of alternative ways to present your information. As a creative speaker, you have the freedom to play and explore and experiment with different forms of communication. It's your presentation and you are free to be as original and creative as you like, as long as what you're doing serves the higher purpose of your presentation and your audience.

Again, a helpful question to ask is, 'How else can I deliver this piece of information?' You could write or draw a picture on a flip chart; create a storyboard; design a poster; use props; give a demonstration; act out a skit; show a video or play an audio clip. There are so many wild and wonderful ways to say what you need to say, and you have the freedom to make use of all or none of them.

Always remember that it's okay to have fun with your content. Experiment with different methods of expressing yourself and your message in a variety of ways. If you're waiting for permission, then you have it. And trust me, your audience will thank you for it.

Your greatest visual aid

Despite everything I've just said in this chapter, there is one visual aid that surpasses all the others: you. You are your greatest visual aid. There is simply no beating a living, breathing human being. Even the brilliance of technology today cannot compete with the brilliance of the human being. There is no software package that can equal your presence, power and personality. A slide can do many things but what it can't do is be honest and vulnerable.

A slide doesn't have a perspective on life that is rich and unique, from which great stories can be told. It can't smile and laugh or have an off-the-cuff joke with the audience. It can't keep talking or smiling as the tears gently roll down its face. It can't reveal something that is deeply personal that is challenging to share. A slide doesn't have courage and it isn't brave. A slide is only a slide and it can never replace the beauty and perfection of a beautifully imperfect human being.

Your gift as a human being is that you can do all of these things and more. And as a creative public speaker it's your responsibility to do these things. All that's needed is a little bit of courage and a willingness to claim your position at the front of the room where the audience can see you and connect with you. You're not doing this to serve your ego; you're doing this as a service to your audience. You have something to offer; a valuable gift that only you know how to deliver. Your slides are just part of the wrapping, the ribbon around your gift. They are not meant to be your presentation at the expense of you. They were designed to support you in your offering and the communication of your message. In all my years of doing this work, I have never seen a PowerPoint slide that is more interesting than the person standing in front of it.

If there's one thing I wish I had the power to do through this work, it would be to invite every public speaker to let go of their slides and take their position at the front of the room as a human being and to remind them to just speak from their heart. After all, that's all any of us wants from another person. Oh, what a gift that would be!

Always, always remember: You are truly your greatest visual aid.

Key 5
Practise Your Delivery

If you look for perfect, you'll never be content.

LEO TOLSTOY, *Anna Karenina*

W hen we think about practising the delivery of our presentation, our focus tends to go immediately to how we are going to present ourselves and our content. We think about where we are going to stand on stage, what we are going to wear, how we are going to sound and what we are going to do with our hands. We might begin rehearsing in front of the mirror or to a trusted friend or family member. We might even record ourselves on camera and watch it back. We rehearse and rehearse and rehearse in the hope of perfecting our presentation. This would seem natural, right? After all, we are the ones delivering a presentation. Yet rarely do we think about the people we are going to be delivering our content to. In other words, we are so focused on practising being public speakers that we don't think to practise being in the audience.

We've all had the experience of being in an audience. We all know it's an easy job. It's certainly easier than being the one on stage doing the talking. It's not like there are training programs and workshops on how to be the best audience member you can be. And audiences today have become extremely demanding while at the same time slightly lazy.

With the abundance of information and content being delivered through so many different channels, expectations of audience members have increased while their engagement levels and attention spans have decreased. Presenters and public speakers have to not only capture the audience's attention immediately, but they have to hold it for the duration of their presentation, which can sometimes be quite difficult when competing against a variety of communication devices. Therefore, before you start practising your delivery, it can help to practise being the kind of audience member you would like to be delivering your presentation to.

Be the audience member you want as a speaker

If you want an attentive, receptive and encouraging audience when you're delivering your presentation – and let's face it, what speaker doesn't – then a good place to start is in your audience. Okay, so what does that actually mean?

Well, let me explain.

I'm proud to say that I'm one of the best audience members you will ever have in your audience. Yep, I'm that person sitting at the front of the room, nodding and smiling and offering other non-verbal signs of encouragement. Why? Because I know what it takes to step out from the crowd and stand in front of that spotlight as a hundred or so pairs of eyes direct their full attention onto you. It's intimidating. Sometimes even terrifying.

Knowing how daunting that can be as a public speaker, when I'm in an audience I always make it my mission to be the best audience member I can be by giving the speaker my full attention. Presence and attention is the greatest gift we can give another person because it says to them, 'I respect you and what you have to say is of value.'

One thing I often see when I'm sitting in an audience is other people texting and playing with their phones. Sure, the world has changed. Today, it's considered acceptable to tweet comments throughout a presentation and yet while the world might have changed, common courtesy hasn't. We owe it to the person standing before us, who has put their heart and soul into preparing a presentation, to give them our full attention. If this is something that you want from your audience when you're speaking, then start by being that kind of audience member. Turn your phone off and give your attention to whoever is standing in front of you.

So how do you rate as an audience member? Are you one of those people who sit at the back yawning, checking your phone? Do you spend the whole time writing notes, or do you just stare blankly at the person on stage? Are you interested or do you lose focus halfway through? Are you someone who likes to hide in an audience? Do you expect the speaker to engage you and hold your attention or do you see the speaker/audience relationship as a two-way relationship? It's important not to expect from an audience what you're not willing to give. Be the audience member you would want in your audience.

Public speaking is a two-way conversation. Even though the person on stage might be doing most of the talking, the audience is constantly giving feedback. This feedback is essential for the speaker. It helps them to know when they are hitting the mark and when they're not.

I know how appreciative I am of an attentive audience. People have a smile on their faces and they are happy to be there, listening to what I am saying. I understand what an honour and a privilege it is for people to give me their attention. As a speaker, it makes my experience on stage that much easier and enjoyable. Therefore when I'm part of an audience I always aim to give the speaker my full attention.

If you want to become a better public speaker, start by becoming a better audience member. Remember it's not easy to stand up on your own in front of a room of people and reveal yourself in ways that you might only do so with your trusted family and friends. It takes courage and dedication. By practising becoming a better audience member, you will start to naturally attract the audience that you have already become. After all, we're all in this together. Whether you are the one on stage or in the audience, we all have a role to play and responsibility to ourselves and each other to bring forth our best self; to be present and open to receiving whatever the other is offering.

If for whatever reason you don't like the speaker or you don't agree with what they are saying, that's okay. We don't have to like everyone and we don't have to agree with everything that someone says. We especially don't have to agree with someone just because they are the one at the front of the room. Yet even if we don't agree with the person speaking we can still show respect in the same way we would hope others would respect us if the roles were reversed. And at some point the roles will be reversed and it will be you on stage. So start practising now becoming the best audience member you can be.

Practising presence not perfection

As I mentioned in Key 2, we are practising to be present in our delivery rather than practising to be perfect. Most presenters will rehearse their presentation over and over in the hope of perfecting their delivery, but this is usually at the expense of their ability to be present in the moment. When you are not present then you are not emotionally available and if you are not emotionally available to your audience then they will not be able to connect to you or your message.

The intention you have for the practise of your presentation will determine the quality of your delivery. If your intention is to be perfect in your delivery then you will sacrifice your ability to be present and emotionally available to your audience. A perfect and polished presentation certainly looks great and can be an entertaining experience but it will always lack depth. The audience is likely to walk away from such a presentation making comments such as, 'That was a really great presentation and the presenter was very impressive. Now what's for lunch?'

When your intention is to be present when delivering your presentation, you open yourself to the moment and whatever might arise. A wonderful example of a speaker who practises presence when they speak rather than being perfect is one of my all-time favourite speakers, the late Dr Wayne Dyer. Dr Dyer was a prolific bestselling author and one of the world's leading spiritual teachers. He spent over forty years travelling the world lecturing and speaking to hundreds and thousands of people, both on stage and through his Public Television Broadcasts in the United States. He said recently in one of his public speaking videos, 'I always think of my presentations as a growth process that I'm continuously going through.'

I've had the wonderful privilege of seeing Dr Dyer speak several times in person but there's one time that stands out in my mind. Dr Dyer was well into his seventies, still travelling the world, speaking to packed auditoriums and sharing his heartfelt wisdom with his audiences. As he stepped onto the stage, he told the five hundred plus audience that he had no idea what he was going to talk about. He stopped preparing notes for his presentations many years earlier, choosing instead to meditate and bring himself into a deep state of presence before stepping on stage.

Dr Dyer went on to speak without notes for four straight hours during which I, and every single person in the audience, remained perfectly still and on the edge of our seats, completely engrossed and focused on every word that left his lips. Dr Dyer spoke with such presence and ease that it was as if every word was being guided *through* him rather than coming from him. Time disappeared as he flowed seamlessly from sharing spiritual wisdom to a personal story to telling a joke and having the audience in fits of laughter. His presentation was more like a song that was being sung from the inner recesses of his heart; a melody that was mesmerising every mind and heart in the room that day. When it was time for a break four hours later, it felt like not a minute had passed. Remember, Dr Dyer had come on stage with no prepared notes or idea what he was going to say.

Dr Dyer didn't just speak with his words, he also spoke with his *being* and it was his presence on stage that had the biggest impact, certainly on me. His presence was so powerful because it brought everyone else in that room into a state of presence also. It was as if the words he spoke were secondary to the message he was sharing. His energy alone spoke volumes. He lived his message and he personified the act of service that public speaking is. It's a service he performed lovingly and continuously for his entire career and I'm grateful to have been present and witness to his presentations.

This realm of creative public speaking is available to all of us, provided we shift our focus from practising perfection to practising presence. Like Dr Dyer, we too can be in a state of presence when we address our audience. We can prepare ourselves to allow the words to move through us rather than having to learn and memorise them. We can trust that this great and infinite intelligence is working through us in the same way it was working through Dr Dyer when he spoke. Wayne Dyer is truly an example of what is possible when we prepare to be present rather than perfect and offer ourselves as a communication tool for whatever message and information is urging itself to be brought forth into the physical realm.

The power of presence is available to all of us right now. It's not something that is reserved for a special few. We all have the capacity and capability to speak from our hearts, to touch the hearts of others through our presence and our words. To access this power, however, we have to be prepared to let go of our need to be perfect and polished. Presence, rather than a well-rehearsed script or set of slides, is the cultivation of this power. We can still be prepared and have an idea of what we want to say while remaining open and available to the words that seek to be expressed through us in each moment. We must be prepared to let go of our notes and trust in the absolute power that is only available to us in the present moment.

Speaking in this form does take practise. Practising presence rather than perfection means practising letting go of having to control every single bit of the process. We can trust the process. Structure is important, but not at the expense of the freedom to allow the inspiration to flow through us. Structure is about feeling supported in our presentation rather than restricted. The more we trust, the more we open ourselves to greater possibilities. We can still have a roadmap of where we are heading, but the moment we step on stage we must be willing to let the roadmap go and allow ourselves to be guided.

Therefore, if you are practising by using a structured script, do so with the intention to eventually let go of the script. Remember no structure is permanent: it's not something rigid to which we are bound for the whole journey. Structure is the support base and can be a guide to where we are going, but it's not the presentation itself. We have to trust that if we know the general direction we are heading and we have some checkpoints along the way, how the journey unfolds is out of our hands. There is simply no way to rehearse the actual journey. We can plan all we like but once we step onto that stage, we are stepping into the unknown. At this point all we can do is trust that we will arrive safely.

Therefore, the first thing we are going to do at this point is ditch the script.

Ditch the script

A common question I am asked is, 'Can I use notes during my presentation?' Of course! You are a creative public speaker; you can do whatever you like. There are no rules. Monica Lewinsky gave a brilliant and powerful TED talk while using notes. Yet as a public speaking coach it's my role to constantly push my clients to challenge themselves, and one of the greatest challenges as a public speaker is to trust in your own abilities and to speak from your heart, without notes. If you are at the stage where you believe you need to use notes or cue cards, do so with the intention to one day let them go. Only you can know when you are ready to do this.

When clients insist on using notes I will ask them why they believe they need them. Responses vary but will usually be along the lines of, 'So I don't lose my place' or, 'So I don't forget what I have to say' or, 'So I feel more relaxed.' These are all legitimate responses, and yet in most instances those insisting on keeping their notes with them during their presentation might look at them once or twice before forgetting that they have them. The truth is they don't need the notes, they just need to trust themselves a little more, something that does become easier over time with practice.

There are also times when presenters hold onto their notes as a way of avoiding eye contact with their audience. Having seen this only too often, such presentations end up being rather monotonous and uninspiring affairs. One example that comes to mind was during an Australian Rules Football Grand Final lunch when three players took the podium to share their experience playing in an AFL Grand Final. The theme for the lunch was 'Live the Dream' and the purpose for the three players to share their experience was to inspire the 500-plus crowd.

Now, imagine growing up with a dream of playing in an AFL Grand Final, running out onto the Melbourne Cricket Ground to the cheers of a 100,000 plus crowd! This is the dream of so many young Australian kids and these three players had all lived this dream. Yet instead of sharing their experience from their heart, they each read from a piece of crumpled paper and never once looked up at the audience. They spoke in flat monotone that held none of the emotion or excitement of the words they were reading. Their presentation was a waste of what could have been a truly memorable experience.

Understandably, the players were nervous. After all, these were professional footballers and public speaking was not necessarily something they were used to doing. Yet unfortunately those pieces of paper they held onto kept them from connecting with everyone in that room who would have loved to have shared in their life-defining moment.

Now let me ask you something: If you were sitting in the audience listening to these amazing players talking about the most memorable moment of their sporting careers, would you care if they fumbled a few words or occasionally tripped over in the delivery of their story? I'm guessing no. Instead, you'd be focused on listening to them describe what it was like to run onto the Melbourne Cricket Ground on Grand Final day. After all, this is not an experience we are likely to have ourselves. It's a unique story because it's someone else's experience of the world. Stories are what is captivating, not the speaker's capacity for perfection in the telling of them.

This is how your audience feels about you. They don't care if you're not perfect in your delivery of your story or presentation. While you always have the option to use notes, the truth is you don't need them. Your aim is to know this for yourself. This may take time and it may require you to use notes for a while as you are learning to trust yourself more, but if you do choose to use notes, make sure they don't come between you and your audience. Always remember, your presence is far more powerful than your words.

In my experience, if someone is presenting on a particular topic it's because they already possess the knowledge and expertise on their subject. While you might still need to rely on your notes, be open to the idea of one day speaking without them. To speak without notes means you've chosen to speak from the heart instead. This is possible for everyone. You only have to believe and trust this is possible for you. The more trust your place in yourself and your abilities as a speaker, the less you will need your notes. And the less you need to rely on your notes or a script, the more present and available you can be with your audience until eventually presence becomes the place you always speak from.

Preparing our instrument

Even in a state of presence, we still have to deliver our presentation through the act of speaking. We do this through the incredible instrument that is our human body. Just as if we were learning to play the piano, it's important to understand how our physical instrument works, in particular, our voice.

Most of us, myself included, take our voices for granted. Until I became interested in the craft of public speaking, I didn't stop to think about how I create the sound necessary to speak to an audience and deliver a presentation. As human beings, we've been blessed with the gift of communication, even though we rarely understand the masterful intelligence that goes into how exactly we communicate, both verbally and non-verbally.

Our ability to use our voice is essential to our ability to perform as a public speaker. Our voice allows us the privilege of delivering our message to our audience. So let's have a quick look at the voice and how it works.

There are three main parts of voice production as outlined by The American Academy of Otolaryngology–Head and Neck Surgery (AAO-HNS): the lungs; the voice box; and your throat, nose, mouth and sinuses. All these aspects go into creating the sound that becomes the words you speak. Let's have a look at them each in greater detail.

1. The Lungs: The Fuel Source

The lungs are your vocal engine. The fuel for your voice comes from the air we exhale. When we inhale, the diaphragm lowers and the rib cage expands, pulling air into the lungs. As we exhale, this process is reversed and air exits the lungs, creating an airstream in the trachea. This airstream provides the energy for the vocal folds in the voice box to produce sound. The stronger the airstream, the stronger the voice. Give your voice good breath support to create a steady, strong airstream that helps you make clear sounds. You can do this by placing one hand on your stomach, just below your belly button and take a couple of deep inhale and exhale breaths. When you can see your hand moving up and down you know you are performing deep belly breathing.

Placing your hand on your stomach as you breathe can also help bring your attention back to your breath if you notice you are feeling nervous. Prior to going on stage, I will always take a few moments to bring my hand to my belly and breathe deeply in and out a few times as this helps to ground my energy and bring my attention back into my body.

2. The Voice Box: The Vibrator

The larynx (or voice box) sits on top of the windpipe. It contains two vocal folds (also known as vocal cords) that open during breathing and close during swallowing and voice production. When we produce sounds, the airstream passes between the two vocal folds that have come together. These folds are soft and are set into vibration by the passing airstream. They vibrate very quickly – from one hundred to one thousand times per second, depending on the pitch of the sound we make. Pitch is determined by the length and tension of the vocal folds, which are controlled by muscles in the larynx.

3. The Resonator: Your Throat, Nose, Mouth and
   Sinuses

By themselves, the vocal folds produce a noise that sounds like simple buzzing, much like the mouthpiece on a trumpet. All of the structure above the folds, including the throat, nose and mouth, are part of the resonator system. We can compare these structures to those of a horn or trumpet. The shape of the resonator tract changes the buzzing sound created by vocal fold vibration, to produce our unique human sound.

Just as professional singers will warm up and tune their voices prior to a performance, creative public speakers must do the same. When our voices are healthy, the three main parts work in harmony to provide effortless voice during speech and singing. If you are going to become a powerful public speaker then you're going to need a powerful voice, one that is healthy and used correctly.

A simple way of doing this is to remember that you can use opportunities throughout your day to practise using your voice correctly. When you are having a conversation with someone, ask yourself 'Where is the sound my voice is making coming from?' If you're shallow breathing then chance are you are speaking from your throat which means over time this will become strained and tired. Instead, bring your attention to your belly and the deeper inhale of your breath. To speak over a long period of time without tiring your voice requires generating air from this deeper place.

In many spiritual traditions, the area of your belly is also considered to be the home of your power, or chi. Chi is energy so if you want to create more power when you speak you must first access this place in your body where it is stored. Again this requires little more than a conscious intention to speak from this place. To get yourself into the habit of doing this, keeping placing a hand on your belly as if to remind yourself that this is where you need to be breathing into and speaking from. Keep doing this until it becomes automatic. To do so is to create a new habit that will support your intention to become a more powerful and engaging public speaker.

Vocal projection

Courage doesn't always roar.

\- **Mary Anne Radmacher**

Many years ago, I attended Tony Robbins' four-day *Unleash Your Power* seminar after a friend offered me a spare ticket. Tony Robbins was described as one of the world's most powerful public speakers and as a public speaking coach, I wanted to see this man in action. After four days of watching Tony on stage, it's fair to say this man is an absolute powerhouse. With over five thousand people in the audience, Tony kept us on the edge of our seats for twelve hours a day for four consecutive days. It was phenomenal. Everything he did, from telling a story to moving around the stage to engaging with someone in the crowd was done with purpose and precision. His body, voice and energy were the instruments he used to change lives.

During one of the activities, Tony had us each write out a mission statement for our lives before inviting someone from the audience to join him on stage and share their mission state-ment with the crowd. Tony picked out a young African Amer-ican guy from New Jersey who introduced himself as Raoul and who, dressed in baggy jeans, T-shirt and sneakers, oozed confidence and cool. Raoul was very comfortable on stage and almost revelled in being in the spotlight.

'Okay,' said Tony. 'Are you willing to share your life mis-sion statement with us?'

'Sure am,' said Raoul, taking the microphone from Tony.

As Tony stepped to the side of the stage, Raoul turned his back to the audience before walking to the back of the stage where he appeared to be taking a few deep breaths and pre-paring himself as if about to perform. Suddenly, Raoul turned around and came running towards the front of the stage, stopping at the edge before yelling into the microphone, 'MY NAME IS RAOUL AND I'M GONNA CHANGE THE WORLD!'

The crowd cheered and Tony returned to centre stage.

'Okay, brother,' said Tony. 'Great job. But can you tell that you didn't hit the spot with your audience?'

Raoul nodded.

'You gotta speak from your heart, brother' continued Tony. 'It's that place deep within you where your true power is. You know what I'm talking about?'

'Yeah' said Raoul, nodding again.

Again, Raoul turned and walked to the back of the stage turning around and this time, sauntering back. Again, he shouted his mission statement into the microphone, yet this time not quite so loudly. 'My name is Raoul and I am gonna change the world!'

Again, the crowd cheered, but this time with less enthusiasm. It was as if everyone in the room knew that Raoul still hadn't hit the mark, even though I don't think we even knew what that 'mark' was. After a few more attempts, Tony asked Raoul to go back to his seat, telling him that he would call him back to the stage later after he had some time to connect with his true voice. 'When you speak from that place of truth within yourself,' said Tony, 'you won't need to shout because we will be able to *feel* every word you speak.'

A few hours later, Tony invited Raoul back to the stage. I noticed there was something different about him. There was a presence and a calmness that wasn't evident before. He didn't look overconfident or out to impress in the way he had before. Tony handed him the microphone before walking off stage but instead of walking to the back of the stage, Raoul simply closed his eyes and took a few deep breaths as the room fell into complete silence. After a short moment, Raoul opened his eyes, looked around the room at the audience before bringing the microphone up to just under his chin and softly and calmly said, 'My name is Raoul and I have a mission to change the world.'

The crowd went absolutely wild!

Tony grabbed Raoul, giving him a big hug as Raoul looked as if he was about to burst into tears. We knew Raoul had hit the mark because we could all *feel* his words. We believed him and as a result he didn't have to shout or yell what he was saying to be heard.

When it comes to the craft of public speaking, there is a huge emphasis on strategies and techniques on how to project your voice to the back of the room so the audience can hear you. Now of course it's important that your audience can actually hear what you are saying. True projection, however, is the energy behind the words rather than the volume they are spoken with. If you want your audience to really hear what you are saying then your words must come from a place of deep truth and honesty. When you speak from this place, you can whisper your words and your audience will hear every single one of them. They will *feel* them.

True projection, instead of shouting or yelling or speaking to the back of the room, is found through your presence. When you are connected to the present moment through your breath and body, you automatically access the power to project your message into the hearts and minds of your audience. Yet this power is only available in the present moment. When you speak with presence, the projection of your voice is not something you will have to figure out how to accomplish. Focus on presence and the projection of your voice will take care of itself. This is your true power.

Maintaining your energy

Have you ever been witness to a speaker who makes it feels as though time has stopped and you have moved into a deep state of presence? There are many speakers today who have this capacity to speak with such presence. I've had the privilege of listening to many of them. One who comes to mind and who has this gift is Matt Kahn.

Matt is a spiritual teacher, a mystic and highly attuned empathic healer. I came across his teachings a few years ago after a friend sent me a clip of one of his 'transmissions' on YouTube. At first I wasn't sure about the guy. He spoke with such calm and clarity but to be honest, I found him unnerving. After listening to him a few times, I realised that I wasn't used to listening to a speaker who was simply so at peace with themselves in front of an audience.

Matt is a wonderful example of someone who speaks entirely from a state of presence, without any of the bells and whistles so many of us have come to expect from public speakers. He even remains seated as he's speaking for his presence and the message he is offering is enough. His purpose for speaking is very clear and the way he speaks to his audience is a clear demonstration of this purpose. Speaking is a tool through which he is able to make a difference and he does it in a very simple and economical way.

In the beginning of my speaking career as a workshop facilitator I would often finish a session completely exhausted. My body would be aching and my throat would feel strained. After a few years I realised that with my energy levels so depleted, there was no way I could keep going like this. To continue speaking on a regular basis, I would have to learn to use my energy more effectively.

One of the ways I did this was by simplifying the way I presented. Based on my nervousness and desire for validation from my audience, I was focused on giving my audience everything I had in the hope they would like me and what I was saying. But being a 'bells and whistle' presenter is exhausting and I learned that less is more. I began slowing down, both in the way I spoke and moved on stage. I connected more deeply with my breath and found that by focusing on becoming more present while on stage, I had more energy. At the end of my presentations, rather than feeling wiped out I began to feel energised. Managing my energy by focusing on remaining calm and present has been essential in my development as a public speaker and I'm sure it will be for you too.

Key 6

Present Your Keynote

M any years ago I was contracted by a multinational company to run a training program across Australia and New Zealand. It was a big contract, and naturally I was nervous. On the morning of the first day of the program, I woke early to go over the presentation, playing it out several times, both physically and in my head. Yet no matter how many times I did this, I couldn't get it to feel right. At the last minute I decided to change a few slides (I only had a few – I promise!) although I didn't have time to run through them. I left my house in a state of panic and upon walking into the conference room I seriously considered faking another last minute trip to New Zealand.

With an hour to go before the attendees were due to arrive I used the time to calm and centre myself through a series of breathing exercises. By the time everyone started arriving, I was in a much more relaxed and focused state of mind. The presentation went well, although it didn't go as well as I would have liked. I never felt completely at ease throughout the presentation. I know this had everything to do with how I had conducted my preparation in the lead up to the presentation and the fact that I had changed my slides at the last minute. As this was in the early days of my career, I wasn't thoughtful about how I prepared on the actual day of the presentation. Instead, I would wing it depending on what I had time for. Over time, it became apparent that this way of preparing for a presentation on the day didn't serve my audience or me.

When I ask people how they prepare themselves on the day of a presentation, the answers vary greatly. Some people prefer not to think about their presentation on the day, others will run through it by reading over a script, others will stand up and run through it in front of a mirror. Some report making last minute changes while others might even throw out what they have and start again from the beginning. While it's important to find out what method of 'on the day' preparation suits you, there are a few things I recommend (throwing out your presentation and starting again on the morning of the presentation is not one of them). In particular, it's important to be conscious of your state of being. Are you preparing in a state of trust or are you preparing in a state of fear?

It's natural to experience nerves or 'butterflies in the stomach'. This is a healthy response to speaking in public. But if we prepare from a place of fear, we are more likely to experience fear when we present. In an attempt to reduce fear on the day of presentation we tend to end up over preparing and creating even more fear than we woke up with.

On the other hand, when we prepare from a place of trust we are more likely to experience the benefits of trust. Rather than going over and over our presentation on the day we are scheduled to present, we might perhaps go over our notes once or twice before turning our attention to becoming present and remembering that we have all the information we need to give the best presentation we are capable of giving. We know the right words will come the moment they are required and as such, we remain open and relaxed.

Just as there are no rules for how you deliver your presentation, there are no rules about how best to prepare yourself on the day. There are guidelines that you can follow that will help you be most effective in your delivery but ultimately, you are an individual and it's up to you to find what works for you. My suggestion is that you focus more on bringing yourself into a state of relaxed awareness rather than on the content of your presentation.

My personal preparation routine continues to change and develop over the years. It's something that's fluid and flexible which I continue to adjust according to my circumstances. On the day of my presentation, while I might run through my words a couple of times, I spend the majority of my preparation time meditating and bringing myself into a relaxed state. My focus is all about feeling comfortable within myself and reinforcing the trust I have that everything I need to deliver my presentation will come to me at the exact moment I need it.

When you focus on trusting in yourself, remembering that you have everything you need to give a great presentation, you are more likely to have this experience when it comes time to deliver your presentation. You are the creator of your experiences based on where you choose to direct your focus, including when it comes to delivering a presentation. It's just like Henry Ford said, 'Whether you think you can or can't – you're right.'

On the day, when you are preparing to deliver your keynote there are three areas you need to focus on. These include personal preparation, keynote preparation and environmental preparation.

Personal preparation

Personal preparation is about bringing yourself into the best state of being in which to present. Personally, I like to keep my routine as close to normal as possible as it helps me stay calm and relaxed.

Firstly, it's important to get a good night's sleep the night before your presentation. If you are over-anxious about your presentation, you will risk waking up in the middle of the night as your brain continues to go over and over it in your head. If this happens, don't resist. That would only guarantee that you wouldn't be getting any more sleep for the rest of the night. If you find you can't sleep the night before your presentation, avoid tossing and turning, and instead lie still with your eyes closed and focus on your breath. By focusing on your breath and slowing it down, eventually you will fall back to sleep.

Upon waking up, it's also important to eat well and try to get some exercise. One little point to keep in mind is to lighten up on any milk intake as milk can create a mucus build up in the throat and sinus making it just a little more difficult to speak and breathe.

It's also a good idea to give yourself as much time as possible in the morning so that you're not rushing and placing unnecessary pressure on yourself. If I'm presenting or running a workshop at a location I've never been to before, I like to arrive at least an hour early as this gives me time to set up the room and connect with my surroundings. If I'm presenting where there is not much to set up, I will always arrive at least thirty minutes before. This still allows me time and space to acclimatise to my surroundings.

Vocal warm up should also be included in your physical preparation. Remember without your voice it's going to be a little tricky to be of service to your audience. Your voice is your instrument and, in the same way an athlete or a musician wouldn't dream of playing before having first warmed up their instrument, so must you. I will usually warm up my voice either while I'm in the shower or driving. It doesn't have to be a super serious activity. You can simply repeat some tongue twisters, stretch your mouth open and closed a few times, sounding out various words and stretch your tongue muscles.

By this stage you would normally have your daily presence practice (as discussed in Key 2), and the morning of your presentation is no different. Find yourself a comfortable spot where you can sit quietly for approximately twenty to thirty minutes, focusing on your breath and releasing any nervousness and tension you might be feeling. I will continue observing my breath until my energy is grounded and I feel centred in my body. I will also do this just prior to going on stage, even if it's just a quick three to five minutes.

If you feel inclined you can also do a quick visualisation exercise once you're feeling grounded and relaxed. With your eyes still closed, bring a vision of yourself standing in front of your audience. Imagine them smiling and nodding and engaging with what you are saying. See yourself gliding around the room, your body moving easily and the words flowing effortlessly. Focus on cultivating a sense of comfort and ease while you are on stage. Hold that feeling for a few seconds before taking a few deep breaths and opening your eyes again.

Whenever I visualise, I will always let the scene unfold naturally. Don't try to control it. If something arises that doesn't look or feel right, simply hold the image in your mind and breathe into it. Wait for it to change, which it will if you're patient. If you happen to notice any faces in the audience that are not smiling or seem resistant, breathe into the image until you can feel their support and acceptance. I will only close my visualisation when I'm happy with how my presentation feels in my mind's eye, and I always take a moment to imprint this feeling in my body.

Lastly, if this resonates with you, I suggest offering a prayer to whatever it is you believe in whether that's God, your Higher Self, Buddha or the infinite intelligence of the universe, surrendering to the idea 'whatever will be will be.' This is something I've been doing for the past few years and I find it very calming. At this point you've done all you can do and whatever happens from this point on is going to be what happens. May as well surrender to it and enjoy the experience.

Keynote preparation

Contrary to popular belief, the time just before you are sched-uled to present is not the time to be rehearsing your presen-tation. It's especially not the time to be making changes. On the day of your presentation, the focus is primarily on getting yourself into a calm, positive and confident state of mind. By this stage, you will have created a powerful and purposeful pre-sentation. Now is the time to let all that preparation you've already done do the work for you.

In my experience, when people feel nervous before present-ing, they focus on content, believing if they just run through it one more time the fear will subside. But as already mentioned, perfectionism is not preparation. Perfectionism is what under-mines people's presentation preparation, especially if it's the focus on the day.

Now is the time to remind yourself that you've done the work and you know your stuff. Any preparation on your con-tent should be minimal with the majority of your focus being to bring yourself into a state of presence. Trust in yourself, but perhaps more importantly, trust in your Higher Self, or God, or Universal Intelligence or whatever you choose to call the invis-ible mystery in which all of life resides, including the outcome of your presentation. Surrender to the unknown and know that whatever happens is exactly what is meant to happen.

Environmental preparation

As I mentioned above, it's a good idea to arrive early just to get a sense of the space where you are going to be speaking, especially if you are new to the space.

The environment in which you present will often vary. The trick is to do whatever you need to do to make the space your own. The more you invest in creating the right atmosphere for yourself, the more your audience will feel comfortable and relaxed as well. It's important for you to do whatever you need to do, within reason, to make the space feel like your own, even if it's just for a fifteen-minute presentation. You might want to move some of the furniture around, adjusting or removing the lectern if there is one, or whatever else you feel needs changing.

I remember seeing a presenter once who spent his entire presentation talking to one side of the room. A table had been placed in the centre of the room for his computer and this made it difficult for him to move around. With the overhead projector attached to the roof, there was no reason for the table to be there. It hadn't occurred to the presenter that he could actually move the table. Such a small detail ended up having a big impact on his presentation because he could only face half his audience, while the other half were forgotten and were therefore less engaged.

One of the first things I like to do when I arrive at a venue is introduce myself to whoever is in charge, making a point to be polite and friendly, as chances are I'll be calling on them for assistance at some point; whether it's to turn up the air conditioning, fix a broken door, fill up the water jugs or locate a flip chart that never arrived (even though it was requested). It helps to have someone close by who knows the venue, just in case things don't go to plan.

The other thing I like to do once I've arrived at the venue is to take a few moments to walk around the room and ground myself in both my body and the space I'll be speaking. Walking around helps me to get a sense of the size of the room and, especially if I'm speaking to a large crowd, helps me to understand where I need to focus my attention and project my voice. As a right-hander, I have a tendency to favour the right side, which means I have to make a conscious effort to direct my attention to my left hand side so that I don't forget about that side of my audience. By walking around the entire space, it serves as a reminder to focus on all of the room rather than just one side of it.

These might all sound like simple and insignificant things but when we're speaking in public, it can be the little things that undo us when they need not. Your environment is there to help and serve you in delivering the best presentation possible. Pay it some of your attention, make friends with it, become familiar with and change what doesn't work.

Working with technology

These days technology is very much part of the modern presentation. While technology will never replace genuine human connection, if you are using it then make sure you are well and truly prepared with it. Technology can be a fickle friend, working one day while deciding to shut down the next. If you use technology, use it only to enhance your presentation. You never want to be in a situation where technology fails (which it's likely to at least once in your presenting career) and you're left with nothing to present.

There's a lot that can go wrong with technology, so it's always a good idea to arrive early to check that the equipment works the way you need it to. If the technology does decide to take a holiday during your presentation – for example the power dies, the screen goes blank or the computer freezes – remember the show must go on. If you can't fix it within a couple of minutes then your only option is to just carry on. This is why it's always a good idea to be prepared to present without technology, keeping in mind it is only there to assist you in your delivery, rather than deliver your presentation for you.

If you get caught out with technology, don't feel you have to hide it from your audience. Chances are they will know something is up anyway. Use it as an experience to connect on a more human level with your audience. Let them in on what's happening. It's natural for things to break down at times. Obviously, it's not ideal but ultimately these things are out of our control so if it happens, surrender to the experience and go with it. See the humour and have a laugh with your audience. If you're okay with something not going to plan, they will be too. It's life. It happens.

Listen to your audience

To listen well, is as powerful a means of influence as to talk well, and is essential to all true conversation.

- Chinese Proverb

During a two-day program I was co-facilitating for a large organisation, one of the company's senior managers marched into the conference room while my colleague Phil and I were presenting. In the middle of our presentation, he demanded to see one of the female participants outside. The woman stood up and left the room as we continued on with the session. Twenty minutes later, the woman came back into the room although it was apparent all was not well. Slowly, she began packing up her belongings.

Phil and I noticed that the group were focused on their colleague and were no longer listening to us. We looked at each other and nodded, silently agreeing to pause the session and ask the woman if there was anything we could do to help. The woman began sobbing and informed the group that she had just been made redundant. On top of this, as the manager of her team of ten people, she had been given until the end of the day to inform them that they too had lost their jobs. Understandably, the woman was devastated.

As she left the room, the mood in the room changed dramatically. Phil and I could see the expressions on people's faces had turned from distress and shock to anger, so we called a short break during which we discussed how we were going to handle the situation. We had two options: we could carry on with the presentation as intended, knowing that we had a certain amount to get through in a specific amount of time, or we could put the session aside, and address the current situation. We decided on the latter and called the group back to explain the change of plan.

This decision turned out to be the right one. The group were clearly distressed, as the incident had triggered their own fears of losing their jobs. Without saying anything, our audience were telling us that they were upset and didn't care about anything we had to say. Were we to ignore these non-verbal signals, we risked alienating ourselves from any chance of connection later down the track. By cancelling the afternoon schedule, we gave the group the space to process and express their emotions around their colleague's redundancy. The following day, the group returned with renewed focus and commitment.

Contrary to how it might appear, your audience is *always* communicating with you. While our audience never said anything to us verbally, they spoke volumes through their behaviour. Fortunately we were able to adjust our presentation for the purpose of ultimately giving them what they needed: time to process events, and the rest of the presentation once they were ready. As a presenter, it's easy to fall into the trap that you are the only one communicating, yet this is not the case. While you might be doing all the talking and your audience is doing the listening, your job is to know how to listen to what they are saying, albeit in a non-verbal way.

In my experience, the best presenters are those who not only know how to listen to their audience, but adapt their presentation and communication style accordingly. A good question to hold in the back of your mind while you're presenting is, *What is my audience trying to tell me right now?* Sometimes we don't ask the question because we don't want to know the answer. After all, it might mean we have to throw out the presentation we've worked so hard on, and instead trust our instincts.

Listen with your senses

As you are the one doing the talking, the way to listen to your audience is with your senses, including your sixth sense. Perhaps one of the easiest ways to listen to your audience is with your eyes. Maintaining eye contact with your audience will keep you in the know about how they are engaging with what you have to say.

Eye contact can be confrontational. There is little more daunting than standing on a stage and looking out into a room with several hundred pairs of eyes staring back. And yet eye contact is exactly what you need to foster, not only to connect with your audience, but to understand what they are trying to tell you. Are they with you or have you lost them? Now, how might you know the answer to this question if you're busy staring into a pile of notes or slides or a computer screen?

This was the challenge for Jason, who has to speak in public on a regular basis as part of his role for the company where he works. Jason approached me because he felt he lacked the ability to command attention from his audience. When I asked him to explain his method of presenting, he told me that before he began speaking, he would first hand out a hard copy of his presentation to everyone in the room. He also had the information on PowerPoint slides, which he would use throughout his speech. He would then talk his audience through each slide, explaining each one in detail despite already having the information in the handouts he had given them.

As it turns out, Jason's problem wasn't his inability to command attention. Jason could command attention just fine. His audience was attentive; it's just that their attention was never focused on him. In fact, he had managed to ensure that they never really saw him since they were always either looking at the notes or the slides. Jason was commanding their attention to be anywhere but on him. What he didn't yet realise was that he didn't want the attention of his audience and, in this respect, he was very successful.

Jason went on to admit that he felt uncomfortable in his own skin and was embarrassed by his weight. He didn't want other people to see him and he struggled to make eye contact with everyone. Thankfully Jason realised that to speak with power and command his audience's attention, he had to be willing to let go of the visual aids that had become more like visual crutches. Jason had to recognise that public speaking was an act of service and that by directing his audience's attention towards him rather than away from him was actually for his audience's benefit rather than his own.

I often hear the trick to overcoming the fear of making eye contact with your audience is to create the impression that you are making eye contact with them. Suggested techniques include scanning the room, looking at the back wall or at people's foreheads, focusing on one person in the audience, imagining people naked or making the letter 'z' across the room as if you were looking at the people in each section of the room. It's almost as if presenters will do anything to avoid making eye contact with the actual people they are there to present to. Yet how can we be of service to people if we can't even bear to look them in the eye?

Eye contact is a critical part of your presentation. You must be able to make eye contact with the people in your audience. Keep in mind, these are just people. They are just regular human beings with fears and insecurities and hopes and dreams, just like you and me. They are not scary monsters who are out to get you and criticize you and bring you down. For the most part, certainly in my experience, audience members are kind. They want to see you do well. They want you to succeed but most importantly, they want to feel connected to you. They want to see you and to be seen by you. And this is only possible when you put down your notes and put away your slides and look your audience members in the eyes.

Although it's not just your eyes that you're listening to your audience with – your emotional awareness will also give you a sense of how your audience is feeling. Being tuned in to the energy of the room is an important skill for a presenter to develop because it can help you manage the delivery of your presentation more effectively. I know when it's time to move or shift the audience's attention to a different focus, because I can feel the energy dipping. If I want to bring the energy back up then I just move to another side of the room, or redirect attention by telling a story, or put up a PowerPoint slide, especially if the focus has been on me for some time.

Always keep in mind, however, that it's natural for energy levels in the room to rise and fall. You're not going to hold your audience's attention the entire time you are speaking. It's natural for people to tune in and out, and for energy levels to oscillate. Yet it's a presenter's job to always be aware of this rising and falling of energy and focus. Ensure it doesn't fall for too long by practising the flexibility to create enough variety and interest in your delivery, helping you maintain focus and engagement until the end.

Let go of outcomes

By letting it go, it all gets done.

- **Lao-Tzu**

Many years ago I read a book during a particularly difficult time in my life. The book was *A Return to Love* by Marianne Williamson and after reading the book three times consecutively, I wanted everyone I knew to have the same life-changing experience I did from reading this book. I went out and bought several copies that I gave away to family and friends in the hope they would love the book as much as I did.

Surprisingly, they didn't. A few read the book and thought it was interesting, some enjoyed it while the majority of people I gave the book to didn't even read it. At the time, I was so disappointed. How could this book not have the same profound effect on others as it did on me? How come my loved ones were not throwing themselves at my feet in gratitude for saving their lives? What on earth was wrong with people?

While I didn't realise it at the time, I was giving people a gift and expecting them to react in the way I wanted based on how I thought it would make me feel. I wanted to be the person who changed their lives by sharing this book and to be recognised and appreciated accordingly. It was as if I *needed* people to love my gift as proof of my worth. Without realising it, I was attempting to use my gift to get something from others in return and I know this because disappointment is always an indication of our expectations not being met.

Naturally, when we give a gift to someone, we want them to love it. Yet to truly give a gift is to not expect anything in return. When we give freely we allow the recipient of our gift the freedom to choose whatever response they wish. They will either like it or they won't. They will find it useful, or they won't. They will think we are great as a result, or they won't. Unfortunately, as much as we would like to and perhaps even try to, we simply don't have any control over how people will respond to the gift we are offering. Our job is merely to give. The outcome is out of our hands.

The same is true for when we present. We have a gift to offer, but the reality is that not everyone is going to like or accept what we are offering. Not everyone is going to agree with you but perhaps most confronting, not everyone is going to like you. Despite our best and most heartfelt efforts, there are times when what we are offering is not going to be appropriate or it's not what people want. This is not something we have control of and the best thing we can do is accept that this is one of the realities of being a public speaker and practise being non-attached.

Non-attachment is *not* detachment. Being detached from something suggests that we don't care about the outcome. As presenters we care very much about our message and our audience, yet when we present from a place of non-attachment, we are more likely to relax into our delivery while knowing the outcomes truly are out of our hands.

The way you do this as a public speaker is to simply focus on doing the best job you can in the offering of your gift. Your message is not going to be accepted by everyone. You can't force people into taking action. You can only offer your message with heartfelt commitment and allow others the freedom to do what they want with it. Just as it's a parent's role to validate their child's thoughts and feelings, even if they differ from their own, as presenters we must remember that our audience has the right to their own thoughts, feelings, beliefs and opinions. We simply can't take it personally. Ironically, people can sense when they are free to feel however they choose and as a result often end up responding to us in a positive and affirming way.

Coping with Criticism

In light of the previous section, we are human and there will be times when we can't help but take other people's opinion personally. I remember many years ago I delivered a presentation to a group of about a hundred people and received positive feedback from about ninety-nine of those people. Yet when I read through the feedback forms I noticed that one person in the audience had expressed his disapproval of my presentation, outlining all the things I did wrong and that he didn't like or agree with. Despite the wonderful feedback from everyone else in the audience, I couldn't take my mind off this one person's negative response.

Thankfully, I no longer worry (as much) about what people think of me or what I have to share. While I would love everyone to like and agree with me, I'm realistic enough to know this is just not possible. When I'm speaking to an audience, my focus is doing my best while staying true to the gift I have to share. I know I'm not going to satisfy every person in the room so I don't try to. This has taken off much of the pressure I used to put on myself and I'm no longer overly concerned if and when I receive negative feedback.

Someone I take great inspiration from when it comes to dealing with public opinion and coping with criticism is best-selling author Elizabeth Gilbert. Elizabeth is someone who has achieved phenomenal success in her career as a writer and has also had to cope with intense levels of criticism. During a difficult time in my life when I was copping a fair bit of negative publicity for a book I had written, I serendipitously clicked onto Elizabeth's Facebook page and discovered an article titled – *Question of the day: How do you cope with criticism?* The timing of her article couldn't have been more perfect and this is part of what she had to say in relation to professional criticism:

'I have a much thicker skin when it comes to professional criticism than personal criticism. I've always understood that it's impossible (and perhaps even unfair) to put something out in the world without allowing other people to have opinions about it. If I get to speak publicly, in other words, then they get to speak publicly, too. Sometimes people's reaction to my work will be warm, sometimes it will be ambivalent, sometimes it will be dismissive, sometimes it will be positively hateful. And thanks to the magic of the Internet, I CAN FIND OUT WHAT EVERYONE IN THE WORLD THINKS OF ME AT ANY TIME OF DAY! (Which you must never do, by the way, unless you are deeply invested in making yourself terribly unhappy.)

'I keep on doing my work anyhow despite criticism. We all have a job in life; writing books happens to mine. It's nothing personal; it's just true. Whatever happens to those books after I publish them is none of my business. People can jump up and down on my books all day, but I still have to make the things. Also, I know this: My critics will write their angry words about me, publish those angry words, tuck their children into bed, have a glass of wine, watch TV and go to sleep … and then never really think about me again. So I shouldn't dwell on them, either. It's just an inhale and an exhale – a natural part of the human process – and then it's done.'

Elizabeth's words are a powerful reminder to keep other people's opinions in perspective. Sometimes feedback can be useful in helping us improve our creative expression, but ultimately it comes down to trusting yourself. You know when you've done a good enough job and you know when you could do better. For me, the only opinions that truly matter are those of the people I love and respect and who only have my best interests at heart. These days I choose to only listen to people whose opinion I respect. Yet ultimately, the most important opinion that matters most to me these days is my own.

To be a public speaker takes courage because you are actively placing yourself outside of the crowd where it's easy to hide and remain small. To place yourself in a position where you are making yourself available to be critiqued and criticised is a trait of a strong and brave person. If you have come this far then it's clear that you are that person. If you believe you have something to offer others and you are passionate about your offering then let that passion be stronger than the opinion of others. I truly believe that if you have a deep calling to speak then there is an audience willing to listen.

Always remember what Wayne Dyer and Elizabeth Gilbert both say: 'What other people think of you is really none of your business.'

Key 7

Prosper Through Speaking

I f someone had told me on that fateful day in Los Angeles as I stood in front of Joe's camera and watched my life flash before my eyes that one day I would be coaching people to be public speakers and that I'd even write a book on the topic, I would have laughed very, very hard and very, very loud in their face. I was anything but a natural public speaker. Yet today is a very different story. Today I can honestly say that I love the craft of public speaking because I see it as a privilege, an honour and an act of service.

Yes, I still get nervous before a presentation. Yes, I still want people to like what I have to say. Yes, I want people to take on board my ideas and suggestions. But I'm no longer attached to these outcomes. Instead, I've come to see public speaking as an opportunity to serve others but also as a way of serving myself. Every time I stand before an audience is an opportunity to expand into an even better and greater version of myself. Public speaking is a continual journey of self-discovery and creative expression. It serves me as much as it serves the people I'm speaking to.

Public speaking can be this for you too. Prospering through speaking is not necessarily about financial prosperity, although that might be part of your experience as you continue to forge your public speaking career. Yet public speaking offers much more than just financial rewards. It's an opportunity to prosper as a human being as well. Rather than being a skill to acquire and develop, public speaking is a process of removing the layers of everything you are not and becoming more of who you are. By challenging yourself to confront and transform your fears, you learn and grow as a person. You develop qualities such as leadership, confidence, courage, authority and influence. My ongoing commitment to my public speaking has made me a more confident and connected person in all other areas of my life.

As you might have already guessed, this is not something that happens overnight. Even with over twenty years of study and practice, I still feel like a beginner. There is an infinite amount to learn and discover through public speaking and as long as you remain committed to it, you will continue to prosper in multiple ways. The key is to keep going and to keep speaking. To continue to prosper through speaking you have to keep finding the courage to keep putting your hand up, keep asking questions, keep volunteering to say a few words and keep seeking out the opportunities to have your message heard. The rewards from doing this are infinite.

To prosper through speaking essentially means to see yourself as a public speaker and to continue your commitment to the role. There is still much to learn and much to gain from the craft just as there is still much that you have to offer and share through speaking. You are now a creative keynote speaker. Here are a few practical ways to ensure you will continue to grow and prosper as one.

Become a professional speaker

A professional speaker is a speaker who is speaking on a regular basis and prospering through these speaking engagements, including financially. If you're only just getting used to the idea of being a creative public speaker, this might sound a little far-fetched. However, becoming a professional public speaker is not as difficult as you might think. It starts with first believing that you have the right and the capability to become a professional public speaker.

As you have already claimed yourself as a creative public speaker, believing yourself to be a professional is just taking this concept one step further. Believing in your ability to be a professional speaker is a case of thinking and acting like a person who is speaking on a regular basis and is someone worthy of getting paid for their speaking efforts. Reminding yourself regularly of your public speaking purpose statement and practising the tools offered in this book will greatly help you to think and act like a professional speaker.

While you might not be speaking all the time, it's important that you are ready and prepared to speak should the opportunity arise. And trust me, the opportunity to speak in public will arise! To continue to develop your confidence and skills as a speaker requires being available to these opportunities, especially since they will often arise unexpectedly and without any prior warning. To be able to stand up and speak at a moment's notice means you first have to trust yourself in being able to do this. You have to believe in yourself first.

As you move through your day remind yourself that you are a creative public speaker and think only thoughts that support your quest to develop your confidence and abilities as a public speaker. If you notice yourself falling back into old thought patterns and habits, quickly bring your attention back to those healthy and supportive thoughts, reminding yourself of all that you have learnt from reading this book. By doing this, when the opportunity to volunteer yourself to speak does arise, you'll be ready to make the most of this opportunity. I know only too well just how easy it is to remain hidden at the back of the room where no one can see you. Yet I can assure you no one ever prospered while hiding in a dark corner.

Seek out opportunities

While opportunities to present will seek *you* out, you also need to be keeping your eyes and ears peeled for opportunities as it's only through the actual *doing* that you will develop your confidence and abilities. If you have a habit of shirking away from public speaking opportunities, then this will feel counter-productive to what you're used to. Yet it's only from breaking out of your comfort zone and learning to put yourself out the front that will enable you to really prosper as a creative public speaker.

One of the easiest ways to do this, and which will quickly build your confidence, is to put up your hand during Question & Answer time during someone else's presentation. Most speakers will have time at the end of their presentation for questions. Putting your hand up and being called on to ask a question gives you the opportunity to stand up in front of a large number of people for only a short amount of time and without all the rigmarole that goes with being the presenter. It means you must take the initiative to put your hand up and by doing this you will find it will build your confidence. This will serve you when it's your turn to be the one standing at the front of the room.

Another way of building your speaking confidence is to be the one to offer to 'say a few words' at friendly social events such as birthdays, engagements, weddings and other celebrated milestones. These events are non-threatening and offer the opportunity to practise some of the ideas and activities discussed in this book. By either making yourself available to be asked to speak or actively volunteering yourself will give you the confidence you need to raise the stakes by looking for and seeking out more professional speaking opportunities.

You can start to seek out more professional speaking by contacting relevant professional associations or networking organisations that are often looking for speakers for their next event. It's always a good idea to experience these events first by signing up to be in the audience and it also gives you an opportunity to meet with the host and inform them of your availability as a keynote speaker. You can also contact Human Resources of relevant companies, offering to host a 'Lunch &

Learn' presentation to their staff. Companies are always looking for new and productive ways to engage their staff and your presentation could be exactly what they are looking for.

Be prepared to step out of your comfort zone. If you're someone who had a tendency to avoid public speaking, to suddenly turn around and seek out opportunities might be confronting at first. Just remember what you have learned by reading this book: public speaking is an opportunity to place before others something that could potentially be of value to them. To speak is an act of service.

Build your speaking portfolio

Every opportunity to speak in front of an audience is an opportunity to build your speaking portfolio. Your speaking portfolio is like a resume of all the presentations you have delivered. As you step into a more professional speaking role, a client will first want to see evidence of your speaking style and ability before booking you. This is especially the case if you are being paid the big bucks!

Thinking like a professional means always thinking about how you can make the most of every opportunity that comes your way. When you deliver a presentation, make sure you get a video copy of it. If your presentation isn't being filmed, then ask a friend or colleague to film it for you. This is so you can put your presentation on your website and other people can see you in action. Remember we're not focused on being perfect here, so don't worry that you might not be as confident or experienced as you might wish to be. Everyone has to start somewhere and every presentation is an opportunity for you to demonstrate your natural abilities and share those abilities with others.

Create a Speak Sheet

A Speak Sheet is like a professional resume except it's only for your professional speaking. It's a detailed document about one to two pages long, outlining who you are, the topics you speak on, your speaking experience and your contact details. This is what you send to potential clients who are thinking about booking you as a speaker for their next event. Your Speaking Sheet should include the following items:

- A brief biography
- Keynote topics (no more than three)
- A brief summary of each keynote topic
- A list of recent clients
- A video link to a recent presentation
- One to two brief client testimonials
- Professional memberships
- Relevant qualifications
- Relevant awards
- A recent professional headshot (no selfies!)
- Your contact details including website

Promote yourself

A Speak Sheet is great to have yet it means nothing if no one actually knows you exist. This means you will have to, dare I say it, *promote yourself*. Oh, I can hear the collective groans and yes, I can relate. Personally, I've resisted the concept of self-promotion and I've really had to work hard to change my attitude towards this activity. I've come to realise that self-promotion is an activity that enables me to be of service to others. If people don't know who I am or where to find me then I'm not able to share my gifts. To be of service we have to be prepared to be seen by others. Promoting yourself therefore means to allow others to see and acknowledge you.

Unfortunately this concept of self-promotion has been well and truly taken over by the self-obsessed and fame-hungry. Yet if we take a look at the original definition of the word 'promote' perhaps we wouldn't find the concept so offensive. The word 'promote' comes from the Latin word *promovere*, which means 'to move forward'. When we actively promote ourselves from a place of service, we are simply 'moving forward'. We are moving ourselves forward and we are also inviting others to move forward via the gifts and information we have to share. You can invest as much or as little time into promoting yourself as a speaker as you wish, keeping in mind that what you put in will be what you get back.

Here are a couple of ideas to promote yourself as a professional public speaker and increase speaking engagements in your specific field:

- Write a blog
- Contribute articles to relevant industry magazines
- Create video content on your website
- Create a regular newsletter
- Set up your own YouTube channel
- Create a brochure outlining your speaking resume that you can send to clients
- Offer to create and contribute content to other websites and organisations in your chosen field
- Sign up to publicity services such as SourceBottle that offer ways for you to promote your services (information in the Resource section)
- Engage a Public Relations agency
- Let your network know that you are available to speak at events
- Ultilising social media such as Linked In, Twitter and Facebook.

So now that you are open to the idea of promoting yourself as a speaker in your area of expertise (or at least a little more open), this is an activity that you will need to do on a consistent basis. It's no use just sending out one brochure and hoping for the best. You have to keep up with it on a regular basis. Keep reminding people that you are now available to speak in public and keep reminding them. Also when you give a presentation, let your network know about it. Over time people will come to see you as the professional speaker you have consistently been letting them know you are. Always remember to keep your marketing material such as your speaking resume, video footage, testimonials and headshots up to date.

Finding an agent

If you're serious about becoming a professional public speaker then it might be worth joining an agency or a speaking bureau that represents professional speakers. There are a number of agencies that represents speakers of varying quality so it's a good idea to do your research and identify the agencies who would be most suited to representing you. Since the professional speaking industry is a highly competitive industry, an agent will be looking for speaking experience therefore it's worth waiting until you have met all the necessary requirements before contacting a possible agency or bureau.

Here are a few things a speaking agency will want to see before signing on a new speaker:

- A Speak Sheet or one page resume
- A list of speaking topics with brief summary on each
- A high resolution professional headshot
- Fee information
- Professional video footage of you speaking
- Audio visual requirements
- Client references (a minimum of three)
- A professional website
- A social media presence

If you don't yet have all of these items ticked off, this list is a great set of objectives for you to work towards and will help you to become the professional speaker you know that you can be. Once you are able to check off each item on this list you are ready to seek out a professional organisation to represent you as a speaker, increasing your capacity to be of services to others through your public speaking.

Getting paid

The reason this section is right at the end of this book is because getting paid is one of the last steps to accomplish when becoming a professional speaker. It also needs to be the last thing on your mind until you are in a position to be paid to speak. For most people, in the beginning at least, public speaking is about challenging yourself, overcoming your fears, recognising the gifts you have to offer and developing your abilities to deliver these gifts in a confident, engaging and natural manner.

There's a common misconception that professional public speaking is a quick and easy way to make some big bucks. We've all heard the lucky person who flies First Class around the world while getting paid tens of thousands of dollars for a thirty-minute talk. While this is an accurate scenario for some people on the international speaking circuit, in most cases these speakers happen to be ex-Presidents, celebrities and world champion sport stars, or they are experts in their field with many years of speaking experience.

To join the ranks of the highly paid, or even paid, professional speakers on the speaking circuit, you will need to invest time and energy into learning and mastering the craft in your unique way while practising and implementing the tools offered in this book. It's important to remember that this particular journey differs for everyone. You might be lucky enough to be paid for your first gig or you might have to offer your services for free while you develop your speaking portfolio. Either way, my advice is to see public speaking as an *addition* to your existing career while taking a long term approach.

When you are starting out, it's common to speak for free. You are gaining experience, developing your speaking portfolio, collecting client testimonials, experimenting with what works and what doesn't and generally figuring out how this speaking business works. When you have gained some professional speaking experience, the next step is to have the client pay for your travel and accommodation. When you are speaking for free or having your expenses paid, it's fair to use the opportunity to promote your business and services such as through the sale of books or other products. I do recommend always checking with the client first.

There's nothing more exciting than receiving your first payment as a public speaker. The first time I was paid to give a presentation I was offered $400. I couldn't believe my luck! At that time, that was how much I was earning in a week. Suddenly a whole world of new and exciting possibilities opened up and despite still being afraid of speaking in public, I was suddenly very motivated to overcome this fear. In the years since, I've continued to develop and refine both my content and speaking abilities and in doing so I've been able to command a fee that reciprocates the value I'm offering. While making money is not the end game, at least it's not for me, it is important to value yourself, your time and what you are offering by charging your clients appropriately.

Essentially there is no limit to how much you can be paid as a public speaker. There are people being paid everywhere from nothing to over a million dollars and everything in between to give a keynote presentation. It's up to you to determine what to charge based on an honest assessment of the value you are offering combined with your experience as a speaker. If you are a celebrity with a household name then you will instantly be able to charge more than the unknown speaker. Also if you are an author and considered an expert in your field then it's likely you can charge more than someone without a book.

There are so many different factors involved in how much you can command as a speaker, here is a brief outline of what you can expect to charge as a professional speaker:

- Free – Speakers who are just starting out, gaining experience and building their speaking portfolio
- Expenses paid – Career and industry speakers who speak on behalf of their companies or industry
- $100 - $1000 – Experienced speakers with interesting and relevant content
- $1000 - $5000 – Corporate facilitators, workshop leaders, Master of Ceremonies, guest speakers at small conferences and events.

- $5000 - $20,000 – Leading experts and headline speakers for corporate conferences
- $20,000 - $100,000 – Celebrities, national CEO's, household names and people with extraordinary stories
- $100,000 plus - International names, celebrities, ex-Presidents, global CEO's and game changers

The world of professional public speaking is a truly exciting one because of the infinite possibilities to grow and develop and become who you came into this life to be. When you decide to invest in being a professional public speaker, there is no limit to how far you can go, how high you can reach and how great you can become. Your success as a public speaker is entirely up to you.

CELEBRATE

Congratulations! If you have come this far, then you truly are a creative public speaker. You have faced your fears and moved beyond them (or at least begun to). You have recognised that public speaking is an act of service and an opportunity to make a difference to others. You have identified the gifts that are uniquely yours and which you are free to share. You have begun to let you creative juices flow, understanding that an engaging presentation is a personal one, anchored in emotional connection. You recognise the importance of structure and the freedom it can give you. You have taken the time to understand your audience and what they need from you. You have prepared your mind and your body to be able to deliver your speech with gusto. You have let go of the need to impress and gain validation from others. You have surrendered to the idea that not everyone is going to accept your gift while knowing it's your job to give it everything anyway. You have come to know that public speaking is a lifelong process and you have committed yourself to the mastering of the craft. You have given it your all and therefore there's only one thing left to do: *celebrate.*

If public speaking has been as great a challenge for you as it has for me, then celebrating your achievements and accomplishments is just as important as anything else mentioned in this book. It takes great courage to face your fears, to stand up in front others and speak your truth. I have the utmost respect for anyone who continues to show up to the act of public speaking, especially when it has been something they have been afraid of. There are literally no limits to what can be achieved and the difference that can be made through the vehicle of public speaking. If you feel a calling to share a message with the world then my hope is that this book will help you to do this. And while you might have reached the end of this book, I assure you that this is just the beginning of a very exciting, wonderful and rewarding adventure.

RESOURCES

Here is a list of resources mentioned in this book:

Videos
Simon Sinek – Start With Why
www.startwithwhy.com

TED: Ideas worth spreading
www.ted.com

Books
War of Art: Winning the Inner Creative
Battle by Steven Pressfield

Speaking Associations
Professional Speakers Australia
Phone: 1300 739 993
Website: professionalspeakers.org.au

Publicity Services
SourceBottle
Website: sourcebottle.com

NEXT STEPS

This book is just the beginning.
If you would like to continue your public speaking journey,
Creative Keynote offers several learning programs.

For more information, please go to
www.creativekeynote.com
or email hello@creativekeynote.com

To stay connected with Hedley Derenzie:
Facebook – Hedley Derenzie (Author)
Twitter - hedleyderenzie
LinkedIn – Hedley Derenzie
Instagram – hedleyderenzie

Email: hedley@creativekeynote.com

ACKNOWLEDGEMENTS

This book wouldn't be possible without some wonderful people. Thank you to Bryony Sutherland, Anna-Carin McNamara, Simon Portbury and Andrew Griffiths. A very special thanks to my mum, Diane Derenzie.

ABOUT THE AUTHOR

Hedley Derenzie is a writer, author and public speaking coach.
She lives in Sydney and is currently
preparing for her next presentation.

www.hedleyderenzie.com

www.ingramcontent.com/pod-product-compliance
Lightning Source LLC
Chambersburg PA
CBHW060300220326
41598CB00027B/4182

9780987550835